Windows Troubleshooting Series

Mike Halsey, MVP
Series Editor

Apress®

Windows File System Troubleshooting

Mike Halsey, MVP

Andrew Bettany, MVP

Apress®

Windows File System Troubleshooting

Mike Halsey
Microsoft MVP
Sheffield, South Yorkshire, UK

Andrew Bettany
Microsoft MVP
York, North Yorkshire, UK

ISBN-13 (pbk): 978-1-4842-1017-8
DOI 10.1007/978-1-4842-1016-1

ISBN-13 (electronic): 978-1-4842-1016-1

Library of Congress Control Number: 2015944104

Managing Director: Welmoed Spahr
Lead Editor: Steve Weiss
Technical Reviewer: Sander Berkouwer
Editorial Board: Steve Anglin, Mark Beckner, Gary Cornell, Louise Corrigan, James DeWolf, Jonathan Gennick, Robert Hutchinson, Michelle Lowman, James Markham, Matthew Moodie, Jeffrey Pepper, Douglas Pundick, Ben Renow-Clarke, Gwenan Spearing, Matt Wade, Steve Weiss
Coordinating Editor: Kevin Walter
Copy Editor: Michael G. Laraque
Compositor: SPi Global
Indexer: SPi Global
Artist: SPi Global

Distributed to the book trade worldwide by Springer Science+Business Media New York, 233 Spring Street, 6th Floor, New York, NY 10013. Phone 1-800-SPRINGER, fax (201) 348-4505, e-mail orders-ny@springer-sbm.com, or visit www.springeronline.com. Apress Media, LLC is a California LLC and the sole member (owner) is Springer Science+Business Media Finance Inc (SSBM Finance Inc). SSBM Finance Inc is a **Delaware** corporation.

For information on translations, please e-mail rights@apress.com, or visit www.apress.com.

Apress and friends of ED books may be purchased in bulk for academic, corporate, or promotional use. eBook versions and licenses are also available for most titles. For more information, reference our Special Bulk Sales–eBook Licensing web page at www.apress.com/bulk-sales.

Any source code or other supplementary material referenced by the authors in this text is available to readers at www.apress.com. For detailed information about how to locate your book's source code, go to www.apress.com/source-code/.

Printed on acid-free paper

Thank you to Annette, for holding the fort at home, and to Elena and Thomas, for letting me camp out in Aachen to write my share of this book.

—Andrew

Contents at a Glance

Contents

About the Authors

Mike Halsey is a Microsoft Most Valuable Professional (MVP) awardee and the author of many troubleshooting books, including *Troubleshooting Windows 7: Inside Out, Troubleshoot and Optimize Windows 8: Inside Out*, and *Windows 10 Troubleshooting* from Apress. He is also the author of other books in the Windows Troubleshooting series.

Based in Sheffield, UK, where he lives with his rescue border collie, Jed, Mike gives many talks on Windows subjects, from productivity to security, and makes help, how-to, and troubleshooting videos under the banner PC Support.tv. You can follow him on Facebook and Twitter at @PCSupportTV.

Andrew Bettany a Microsoft Most Valuable Professional (MVP) awardee since 2012 (Windows IT Pro) and a Microsoft Certified Trainer, is technical editor of several titles and coauthor for Microsoft Press of *Exam Ref 70-687: Configuring Windows 8* (2013) and of Microsoft Official Curriculum courses 20687D, 20688D, and 20689D (2014). He is the author of multiple books in the Apress Windows Troubleshooting series.

A regular speaker at IT professionals' events and at TechEd conferences in North America and Europe, Andrew also devotes time to comanaging the UK-wide community "Windows User Group" and running the University of York IT Academy.

He loves to write, travel, and enjoy the countryside and lives on a smallholding close to York in North Yorkshire (UK) with partner, Annette, and young son, Tommy.

About the Technical Reviewer

Sander Berkouwer (MCITP, MCSE, MCT) is a Dutch IT professional with more than 15 years of experience with projects in large IT environments. He is a contributing blogger at the DirTeam.com/ActiveDir.org weblogs (blogs.dirteam.com) and the founder and owner of ServerCore.Net. Since 2009, Microsoft has awarded Sander with the Most Valuable Professional (MVP) award, and since 2011, he works part-time as an IT Professional Evangelist for Microsoft Netherlands.

Windows Troubleshooting Series

When something goes wrong with technology it can seem impossible to diagnose and repair the problem, and harder still to prevent a recurrence. In this series of books, we'll take you inside the workings of your devices and software, and teach you how to find and fix the problems using a simple step-by-step approach that helps you understand the cause, the solution and the tools required.

Series Editor
Mike Halsey, MVP

A Microsoft Most Valuable Professional (MVP) since 2011, Mike Halsey has many years of experience in helping people understand and get the very best from their PCs. Based in Sheffield, UK, where he lives with his rescue border collie, Jed, Mike gives many talks on Windows subjects from productivity to security, and makes help, how-to, and troubleshooting videos under the banner PC Support.tv.

Apress®

Introduction

As I write this introduction, the hard disk on which I have Windows 8.1 installed consists of no fewer than 440,000 files that take up 240GB of space. When all my installed software and apps are removed from this, Windows itself is still enormous, and this is where the complexity of modern operating systems can present problems.

There are tens of thousands of files and hundreds of folders in a basic, new installation of Windows. Many of these help maintain compatibility with older software and hardware; many more exist just to make sure our PCs are able to boot to the desktop.

When you add in hardware drivers, win32 and store apps, and the multitude of temporary and configuration files that make everything work, finding, diagnosing, and repairing problems can be very complex indeed.

Whether you're repairing the Windows boot system, fixing problems with a corrupt underlying file system, or managing the permissions or encryption associated with an individual file, this complexity can quickly become apparent. That's what this book helps to solve. Think of it as your master-class guide to the most complex operating system on the planet.

The tools and utilities that exist within Windows to help repair problems with files, folders, and file systems are extensive and powerful, and a whole range of third-party utilities also exist to ensure that your time with Windows can be trouble- and worry-free. In this book, we'll detail everything you need to know.

CHAPTER 1

■ ■ ■

An Introduction to the Windows File System

Performing a search on the files that make up my own Windows installation, plus software apps and utilities, you'd be unsurprised, I'm sure, to hear that Windows is reporting that there are more than half a million files in almost 80,000 folders on my C: drive, all taking up a whopping 182GB of space.

It's understandable, then, that when problems arise with a Windows installation or installed software, many people find it difficult to know how to begin diagnosing and repairing the problem, and it's because of this type of complexity that the reimage has become the de facto route for repairing a PC.

Often, though, finding and repairing the actual cause of the problem can be significantly faster, especially when you factor in all the updates, installs, and configuration that will have to be made after a reimage—and that is itself a barrier to valuable productivity for the end user.

In this book, then, we'll guide you through the minefield of the Windows file structure and your PC's file system. We'll show you how to work with, manage, and maintain the critical files that make up the Windows OS. We'll detail how to keep user files behaving themselves and take a deep dive into what's what in the jungle that is your PC's hard disk.

An Introduction to File Systems

Before you can copy files and folders of any type onto a hard disk, they need to be formatted with a designated file system, and there have been a few on PCs over the years.

Think of a file system as a database structure in which files and folders are kept as records that are indexed by a central catalog. This database maintains the files and folders, storing the locations of where one ends and the next begins on the physical disk, managing the storage of new files while also providing for more complex operations, such as the splitting of a single hard disk into separate "logical" partitions.

FAT (File Allocation Table) was where it all began back in the early days of DOS. Ahead of its time, it was a 16-bit, and, later, 32-bit, file system (though only 28 bits were used) that was originally designed to manage floppy disks. Transported to mechanical

© Mike Halsey and Andrew Bettany 2015
M. Halsey and A. Bettany, *Windows File System Troubleshooting*,
DOI 10.1007/978-1-4842-1016-1_1

hard drives, it formed the foundation of Windows for many years. There were limitations, however, primarily with its 32-bit structure. These meant that hard disks and files could only be a maximum size of 4GB and that fudges and workarounds had to be found to accommodate anything larger.

Microsoft's NTFS (New Technology File System) was the answer. First introduced in 1993, it's still the foundation of our PC hard disks today. It supports significantly larger disks and higher volumes of files than FAT, while also supporting provision for encryption and other security technologies. It is also more robust and reliable than FAT, making it far less prone to the corruption that caused PC users so many headaches back in the days of Windows 3.1, 95, and 98.

While NTFS is the default file system for Windows, you may occasionally encounter other file systems, though these are far less likely to require troubleshooting, due to the nature of how people use them. UDF (Universal Disk Format) is commonly used for CDs, DVDs, and BluRay discs. exFAT is a rebuilt, and backwardly incompatible, portable file system designed for devices such as USB flash drives.

Then there's ReFS, Microsoft's next-generation file system, already implemented in Windows Server 2012 and Windows 8, and inevitably coming to the PC at some point after that for use in specific scenarios requiring a relational file system. ReFS takes the system introduced by FAT and refined by NTFS to the next level, with built-in integrity checking that makes the CHKDSK disk-repair tool obsolete, and built-in support for the multi-terabyte disks and RAID arrays that are already becoming commonplace.

Resilience and robustness are crucial in a modern file system. We need to be sure that we can purchase that new 8TB hard disk, plug it into our PC, format it, and copy files back and forth for years without incident. Just like anything else on a PC, however, corruption can be caused by anything from an electrical spike to a software glitch.

Table 1-1. *Windows version with their year of release*

File System	Year Introduced	First Used In...
FAT (8-bit)	1977	MS Basic-80
FAT12	1980	QDOS, 86-DOS
FAT16	1984	PC DOS 3, MS DOS 3
HPFS	1988	OS/2
NTFS 1	1993	Windows NT 3.1
UDF	1995	
FAT32	1996	Windows 95 Service Release 2
HFS Plus	1998	Mac OS 8.1
NTFS 3.1	2001	Windows XP
FATX	2002	Xbox
exFAT	2006, 2009	Windows CE 6.0, Windows XP SP3, Windows Vista SP1
TexFAT	2006	Windows CE 6.0
ReFS	2012, 2013	Windows Server 2012, Windows 8

The Windows File and Folder Structure

Sitting on top of this file structure is Windows itself. The Pro version of Windows 8.1 that I have running in a VM currently is 12.8GB in size, with over 74,000 files in more than 17,000 folders. This is without even a single additional piece of hardware or software being installed.

So, how do you navigate your way around this file and folder structure, and what's important? Let's take a look, then, at what's most important in your Windows installation.

Initially, on opening your Windows drive, you will see four or five folders (Figure 1-1): a log folder, one or two programs folders (depending on whether you are running the 32-bit or 64-bit edition of Windows), one where your user profiles and files are stored, and one for Windows itself.

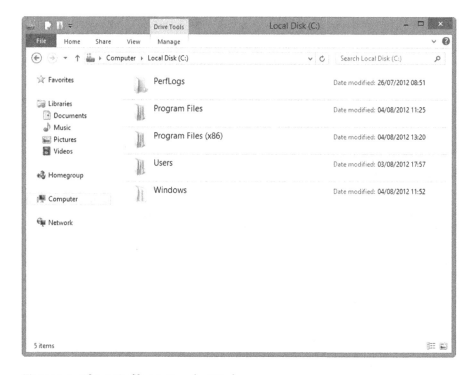

Figure 1-1. *The main file structure for Windows*

There's actually more hidden away here, however, as showing hidden and protected operating system files will display virtual memory paging files, a hibernation memory dump file, and boot system files (see Figure 1-2).

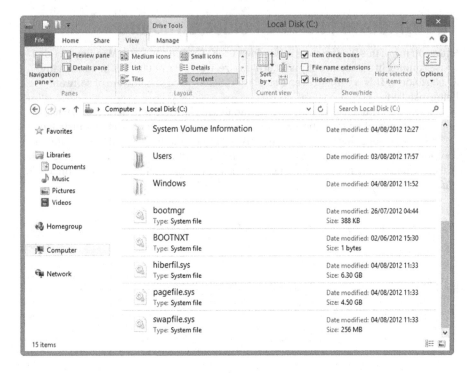

Figure 1-2. *Hidden system files in the Windows root*

Within the Windows folder lies most of the complexity, so we'll begin here (see Figure 1-3). There are several crucial and important folders within the Windows folder that you must know about.

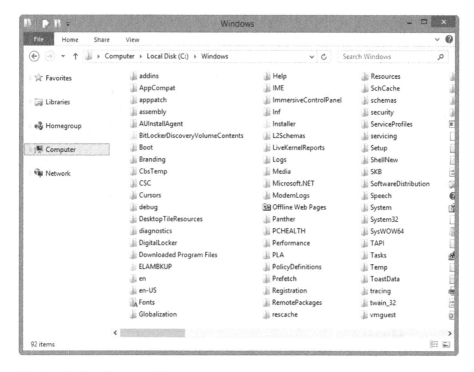

Figure 1-3. *The Windows folder contents*

The first to mention is the one that causes the most confusion: WinSxS. On my own PC, it's a massive 7GB in size, larger even than a base installation image of the OS itself.

It's common, then, for people to believe it's clogged with temporary files and can be deleted. In fact, it's crucial to the operation of Windows and is the largest folder on your hard disk for a good reason.

WinSxS contains all the files necessary to maintain compatibility with hardware and software on your PC. One of, if not the biggest, strengths of Windows is its capacity to maintain compatibility with hardware and software dating back to the early days of DOS.

While other OS developers such as Apple did away with legacy compatibility long ago, Microsoft recognized its importance to the business community. Windows, like any other operating system, includes thousands of utilities that allow software and hardware developers to do everything, from communicate with the OS and different hardware to display windows on your screen.

The files used to accommodate developers are called DLLs (Dynamic-Link Libraries) and they come with the file extensions .DLL and .OCX (the latter additionally containing ActiveX controls) and .DRV to maintain compatibility with legacy hardware.

DLLs (I'll use the term generically here) are cmdlets and utilities that perform everything from putting the minimize, maximize, and close buttons in the correct place on windows to managing ribbon and other interface elements and communication, and they exist so that developers don't have to keep writing these things themselves every time they release a new software package or piece of hardware. People like me who used the famous WordPerfect 5.1 word processor in DOS might remember, for example, that it came with disk after disk of its own printer drivers.

Over the years, there have been many versions of DLLs, as they've been updated, but Microsoft eventually hit a problem whereby one software or hardware package would call a specific version of a DLL at the same time as something else would call a different version. Despite the version numbers for the DLLs (let's say 1.0.0.2 and 1.2.2.4) being different, the file names remained the same, and, consequently, incorrect DLLs that would cause incompatibilities, crashes, and even a Blue Screen of Death were sometimes called.

The solution to this was introduced with Vista and called the Windows Side-by-Side folder, or WinSxS. This folder would store all the different versions of DLLs that were installed by software and hardware packages and allow those packages to always call the correct versions.

Resultantly, the WinSxS folder is pretty huge on any PC and also completely essential to the operation of Windows, your software, and your hardware, and it should not be trimmed or deleted.

The main folders within the Windows folder that are important to the operation of Windows, your software, and hardware are the following:

- **Boot**—This folder contains files necessary for starting the OS. Much more detail on the Windows boot files will appear in Chapter 7.

- **Debug**—This folder contains error logs.

- **Fonts**—The main repository for fonts installed in Windows.

- **Globalization**—Contains language packs, dictionary files, and other files relating to globalization and location.

- **Media**—Contains audio and video associated with the OS, such as Windows sounds.

- **Prefetch**—The Windows Prefetch system loads commonly used files and Windows components ahead of you actually opening them, trying to anticipate what apps you will want to use, so as to speed up loading. The contents of this folder can safely be deleted if the cache becomes corrupt, and it will be rebuilt the next time Windows starts.

- **Resources**—Contains the ease-of-access and other themes for Windows.

- **Software Distribution**—This is another folder the contents of which can be safely deleted. It contains temporary files and settings for Windows Update. If the contents of this folder are deleted, Windows Update will be reset, meaning that any hidden updates will again be visible, and your custom preferences for when updates are installed might be lost.

- **System Volume Information**—This folder is used by the System Restore feature and contains archived and encrypted versions of critical system files, the Windows Registry, and other files pertinent to the safe and smooth operation of the PC. There is a System Volume Information folder on every disk or partition on your PC (except removable media). If you delete it, you will delete all the System Restore points for that drive.

- **System32**—This is the repository of Windows operating system files, and the whole OS is stored in here.

- **System32\Config**—This folder contains the main Registry files for the OS. Additional .dat Registry files can be found in the %userprofile%\ntuser.dat and %userprofile%\AppData\ Local\Microsoft\Windows\ folders.

- **Web**—Contains imagery for your lock screen in Windows 8 and your desktop wallpapers.

- **Program Files and Program Files (x86)**—These folders, found in the root of the Windows install drive, contain all your installed desktop software (not Windows store apps). The Program Files (x86) folder will only appear on 64-bit installations of Windows, on which it will contain all 32-bit software, leaving all 64-bit software in the Program Files folder.

- **Program Files\WindowsApps**—This folder contains all your installed Windows Store apps. It is protected by the highest levels of security in the operating system and cannot be opened, even by an administrator.

- **SysWOW64**—This folder contains files necessary to maintain software and driver compatibility between 32-bit and 64-bit PC systems.

- **MSOCache**—Found in the Windows root folder, this will only appear on PCs on which Microsoft Office 2007 or later versions have been installed. It contains installation files copied from the CD, DVD, or other installation media for Microsoft Office, and these files are used to repair the Office Suite in the event of a problem.

- **ProgramData**—Also found in the Windows root folder, this contains application data for all the users on the PC and is a large folder (3.6GB on my own PC). This application data is not user-specific and can be used by all user accounts. It should not be deleted.

- **Desktop.ini**—This isn't a folder, but a file found within every single folder on your hard disk. It contains customization options for how that folder is to be displayed in File Explorer (Windows Explorer in Vista and Windows 7). Should those customizations become corrupt, you can delete the appropriate Desktop.ini file to reset them.

The Users Folder

The Users folder contains a sub-folder for each user account on the PC, including domain profiles, and a Public folder for documents that are shared between users. Additionally there is a hidden *Default* folder that contains settings used when a new user account is created.

Within each of these folders are the document and other shell folders for the user, created both by Windows (Documents, Pictures, Favorites, etc.) and third-party software (such as the Intel and Creative Cloud Files folders seen in Figure 1-4).

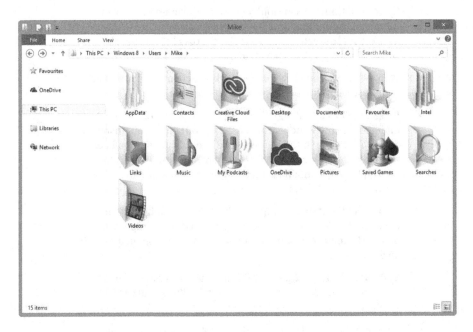

***Figure 1-4.** The Users folder contents*

The AppData folder contains program settings that are unique to that user, and this is another very large folder on the PC—a whopping 21.5GB on my own PC. Within the AppData folder are three sub-folders.

- **Roaming**—Known by the shortcut %appdata%, this contains data and settings that can move with your user account, such as when the user is on a domain. This folder has the ability to sync with a server.

- **Local**—Known by the shortcut %localappdata%, this sub-folder contains the data and settings that cannot move with your user profile and are tied to that PC. This includes browser temporary files, files that are too large to sync with a server, and settings specific to locally installed software. This folder contains the user's *Temp* and *Temporary Internet Files* folders.

- **LocalLow**—This contains data that cannot be moved but that has lower-level access, such as a web browser used in protected or privacy mode.

Windows Log Folders

I mentioned earlier in the chapter that there are folders that contain log files for the OS. These log files can be opened and read as they are stored in plain text and can be used to help diagnose problems with a PC or Windows installation.

- **Windows\Logs**—This is one of the main log folders for a Windows PC and contains log files for many key Windows components. Indeed, Windows scatters log files in many locations, so you may even find some in the root of the Windows folder, such as `WindowsUpdate.log`.

- **PerfLogs**—Located in the root of your Windows drive, this stores Data Collector Set and log files created by the Windows *Performance Information and Tools* and *Performance Monitor* utilities. This data can be deleted if it is not needed. Unless a user specifies that data should be stored on it, this folder is empty in Windows 8 and Windows 10 and only contains Windows Experience Index data for Vista and Windows 7.

- **Debug**—Contains log files, such as those seen in Figure 1-5, created when Windows debugs applications and service crashes and when certain actions are performed, such as installation and running of the Windows Malicious Software Removal Tool. You can safely delete the contents of this folder.

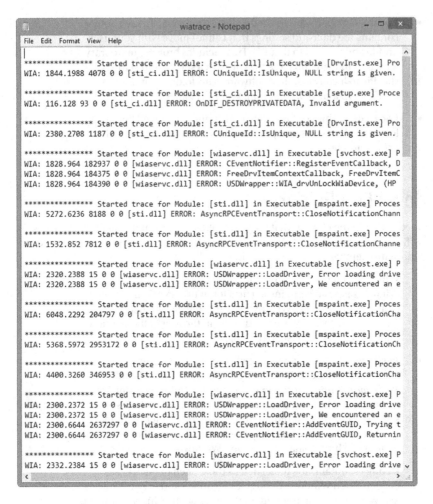

Figure 1-5. *A typical Windows log file*

■ **Note** Blue Screen of Death (BSOD) log files can be stored in several locations. Normally, they are found in the root of your Windows drive; however, in some instances, they can be found in the Windows\System32 folder. A BSOD log file will be called MEMORY.DMP.

- **Minidump**—This is a folder in C:\Windows that can contain crash reports created by applications on your PC. This can include BSOD reports. These files have the extension .dmp.

- **%LOCALAPPDATA%\CrashDumps**—Contains crash dump files pertinent to a specific user. These are stored in the AppData\Local folder of the user.

■ **Note**   .dmp files are not stored in plain text and cannot easily be read in Notepad. You can read .dmp files clearly by installing compatible software such as the Windows Driver Kit (WDK) or Windows Software Development Kit (SDK), both of which are available as part of Microsoft Visual Studio. You can also download the debugging tools for the SDK separately and should search online for the SDK specific to your version of Windows.

Summary

While the main file and folder structure for Microsoft Windows might appear daunting in its size and complexity, there are, as has been detailed in this chapter, only a few folders you will ever want to access, and the files and data you will have to troubleshoot and repair problems are straightforward to find.

As for the rest of the Windows folder, this contains the guts of the Windows operating system itself and should only be accessed should you need to repair the OS on a file-by-file basis, as we shall cover in Chapter 9.

CHAPTER 2

■ ■ ■

Understanding Windows File Systems

Are you new to Windows or are you a seasoned sysadmin? If you remember DOS and pre–Windows 2000 operating systems, you should have a head start on those who have experience only of Windows 7 and later versions. Even if you have many years' experience using Windows, we will introduce some new file system features that are currently available in the newer versions of Windows.

It is not only Windows that relies on a stable file system. Applications and, more important, you rely on a consistent, reliable, and secure storage system for your files. Wherever corruption occurs, there is most likely data loss, and this can be both time-consuming and inconvenient to recover but also costly in terms of data recovery and regeneration where a backup is not available.

In this chapter, we will review disks and partitions, the current file systems available, discuss troubleshooting tools, and look ahead to some of the new technologies that are emerging.

Windows File System Components

- Disks

- Partitions

- File Systems

- Tools

Disks

While the majority of disks installed in PCs at the moment are traditional SATA (Serial ATA) drives, the current speed king is the SSD (solid-state drive). SATA (and its predecessors IDE, PATA, and SCSI) are still available and have proven excellent reliability. Often when repairing and upgrading PCs, many older drives have been proven to be in reliable operation for decades, due to their high build quality.

© Mike Halsey and Andrew Bettany 2015
M. Halsey and A. Bettany, *Windows File System Troubleshooting*,
DOI 10.1007/978-1-4842-1016-1_2

However, just as the need for bigger and faster drives has always meant that new innovations, such as increased disk platter density, greater buffer memory, or direct memory access (DMA), will force older drives to become obsolete, the performance offered by the SSD drive is revolutionizing the hard-drive industry and enabling new devices and form factors to be created.

In relation to troubleshooting, I have often witnessed a user complain about the speed of a particular device, but speed is always relative to the comparison being made.

To indicate the relative speeds of drive technologies compare the drives in Table 2-1.

Table 2-1. Drive Technology Transfer Speeds

Drive Technology	Transfer Speed (maximum)
IDE/ATA	2MB/s
Ultra-ATA	133MB/s
SATA 1.0	157MB/s
SATA 2.0	300MB/s
SATA 3.0	600MB/s
SSD	770MB/s*
SATA 3,2	1969MB/s

Plextor M6e Black Edition SSD boasts sequential read/ write speeds up to 770/625MB/s (December 2014).

Currently, SSD drives are disadvantaged by being significantly more expensive than traditional hard drives, but their advantages include

- No mechanical or moving parts

- More robust against physical damage

- Increased mean time between failure of 1 million hours (vs. 750,000 for SATA)

- Extreme performance for both read and write

- Ability to fit standard 2.5 or 3.5 drive enclosures

- Utilize standard HDD connectors, with the most common being SATA connections

- Significantly lighter than traditional drives

Small footprint mSATA and M.2 form factors (2014 onwards) With the emergence of the SSD, several laptop manufacturers implemented a dual drive approach whereby they would implement a small SSD drive (i.e., 32GB) for use by the operating system and then use a larger (such as a 750GB) SATA drive for data and programs. With the reduction in SSD pricing, this practice is less common.

■ **Note** For comparison, a USB 3.0 drive (which uses a Super Speed Bus) has a maximum throughput of 5Gbps.

With modern tablet devices now using SSDs as standard, there is an acute need for space conservation and careful utilization, due to the smaller space often offered by an SSD. Often, the drive capacity is as little as 32GB, which can leave precious little space after taking account of the operating system and program files.

We have discussed how it is possible to store data on a second drive or partition. You can also force Windows to move the location of one or more user folders to a different location, such as moving your Downloads folder to a second drive, or even an external SDHC card.

To change the location of your Downloads folder, heed the following instructions:

1. Insert your SDHC (optional).

2. Open File Explorer.

3. Select Downloads.

4. Click Properties from the ribbon.

5. Click the Location tab.

6. Click Move and then select the new location on your SDHC card for the Downloads folder.

7. Click OK and then click Yes to confirm that you want to move the files.

■ **Note** Windows 10 will allow installed programs to be moved to an external SDHC card.

Partitioning Disks in Windows

Before we can even format a drive or disk (the words can be used interchangeably) with the file system of our choice, we must first partition the physical disk, so that it can accept the file system. Once formatted, the disk is ready for the operating system to use the available space for storage.

The traditional approach of Microsoft (and original equipment manufacturer [OEM] system builders) has been to ship PCs that contain only one hard drive, and this is partitioned as one drive, on which Windows is installed. This is acceptable for the majority of end users, but for some, one partition is not desirable, and they will often reinstall or reconfigure the drive to meet their requirements.

In Table 2-2, we outline the various reasons and benefits that can be obtained through partitioning a disk.

Table 2-2. *Reasons and Benefits to Partition a Disk*

Reasons to Partition a Disk	Benefits
Create separate areas for system and user data	Where data is stored locally (i.e., on the system), it is best practice to isolate it from the operating system. This can be for ease of backup. In the event of a system crash, only the system partition would have to be reinstalled.
Optimize performance	It is possible to increase system performance by relocating key system files (such as swap, paging, and print spooling files) to partitions (or, indeed, separate disks), away from the system storage.
Dual or multi-boot environment	Originally dual booting required the user to store the alternative operating system on a separate disk drive. This would allow multiple operating and file system combinations (such as Windows 98/FAT32 and Windows XP/NTFS) to coexist on the same PC.

■ **Note**   Modern implementations of dual/multi-boot allow the system to boot directly to a VHD that contains the operating system, without the need to partition the hard drive. Effectively, the VHD is a separate self-contained drive, stored as a VHD file on the hard disk.

Rather than simply dividing a disk into multiple partitions (also known as volumes), we are witnessing a move away from this trend and regressing to the concept of a single use for each disk. Systems are now increasingly being configured with multiple drives—one for the system drive and others for the data. Although beyond the scope of this book, Microsoft Azure virtual machines are provisioned by default with a system and a second virtual disk (though the second drive is not recommended for production use, as it is for temporary storage only).

Since the beginning of computing, the size of everything to do with computers just keeps increasing. It is very easy to become lost when discussing size within computing: do you know the difference between a petabyte and an exabyte? We thought the simple summary in Table 2-3 may serve as a useful reminder. (There are even bigger numbers, but we stopped at exabyte!)

Table 2-3. *File Sizes and Nomenclature*

Quantity	Metric	Equivalent
1024 bytes	1024	1 kilobyte (KB)
1024KB	1,048,576	1 megabyte (MB)
1024MB	1,073,741,824	1 gigabyte (GB)
1024GB	1,099,511,627,776	1 terabyte (TB)
1024TB	1,125,899,906,842,624	1 petabyte (PB)
1024PB	1.15×10^{18}	1 exabyte (EB)

■ **Note** Often you will see speeds referred to as MBps or Gbps. You have to be careful to note the subtle difference between a lower- and uppercase *B*, as it is very significant. Take, for example, SATA 1.0 disks, which have a data throughput of 1.5Gb/s, and SATA 2.0 disks, which have a throughput of 300 MBps. Which is faster? Whenever you see a *B* this refers to a "byte," and when you see a *b*, this refers to a "bit." There are 8 bits per byte, so 300MBps is the same as 300 × 1,048,576 × 8 bits, or 2.34Gb/s

---

MBR vs. GPT Partitions

Windows offers two different disk-partitioning options: Master Boot Record (MBR) and Globally Unique Identifier Partition Table (GPT). GPT is only supported since Windows Vista/Windows Server 2008 (though x64 versions of XP and Server 2003 could also use GPT).

When deciding which partition system to use, refer to Table 2-4, which compares the two.

Table 2-4. *Comparison Between MBR and GPT Partition Systems*

MBR	GPT
4 partitions per disk	128 partitions per disk
Less reliable on modern drives	More reliable on modern (larger) drives
2 terabyte (TB) maximum partition size	Support for very large disks—i.e., up to 18 exabyte (EB) disks
Legacy flat database structure	Improved data structure integrity with CRC32 fields
No built-in redundancy	Creates primary and backup partition tables for redundancy
Bootable from BIOS	Bootable only if the device uses the Extensible Firmware Interface (EFI) Basic input/output system. (GPT data disks are accessible via BIOS.)
All removable drives, such as SDHC drives, USB thumb drives, and USB disks use MBR partitions	Not available for removable media
MBR disk can be converted to a GPT disk	GPT disk can be converted to a MBR disk once all partitions are removed.

You should see from the preceding table that despite some of the excellent features of GPT disks, there are also some significant limitations. The vast majority of Windows installations use the MBR method, as it is commonly known and most widely supported. Most users currently do not have the enhanced requirements that GPT offers, although with the emergence of UEFI as the replacement for BIOS (and UEFI with support for Secure Boot is part of the hardware specification for Windows 8), future versions of Windows will utilize GPT.

Assuming that you are looking to modify or add partitions to your system, the primary built-in tools for performing disk-related tasks are as shown in Table 2-5.

Table 2-5. *Tools for Performing Disk Management Activities*

Tool	Comments
Disk Management (`diskmgmt.msc`)	Administrative graphical user interface (GUI) tool, allows majority of disk and partitions actions. Local and remote use
DiskPart (`DiskPart.exe`)	Command line utility allows all disk and partition tasks and limited scripting. Local use only
Command Prompt	Limited to basic and legacy disk tools
PowerShell	Allows all disk and partition actions, locally and remotely. Extensive scripting abilities

Modern versions of Windows introduced additional functionality to the management of disks, including the ability to

- Easily create and convert between partition types
- Resize partitions through extending and shrinking

To partition a newly created disk to GPT, you would take the following steps:

1. To open Disk Management, type `diskmgmt.msc` (or search for Disk Management in the Start screen).

2. Right-click the new disk (or new VHD) and select Initialize Disk.

3. Choose MBR or GPT, as shown in Figure 2-1.

4. Click OK.

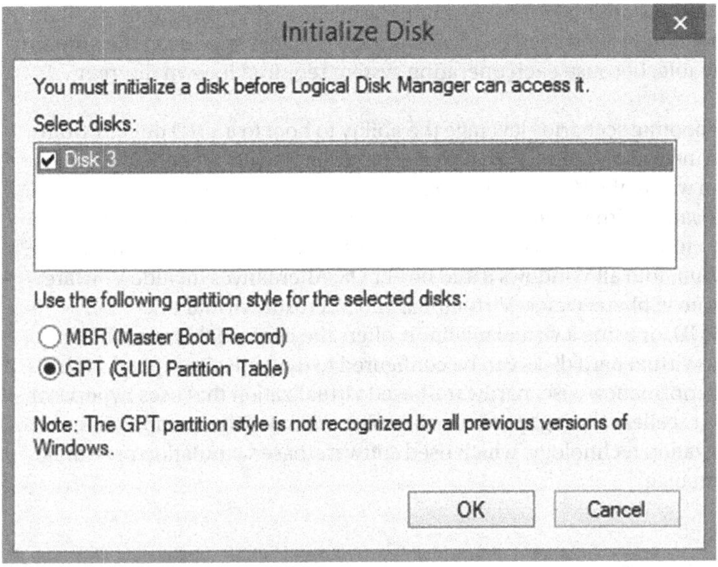

Initialize Disk

You must initialize a disk before Logical Disk Manager can access it.

Select disks:

☑ Disk 3

Use the following partition style for the selected disks:

○ MBR (Master Boot Record)
◉ GPT (GUID Partition Table)

Note: The GPT partition style is not recognized by all previous versions of Windows.

[OK] [Cancel]

Figure 2-1. Initializing a GPT disk

■ **Troubleshooting Tip**   If you have to know what method of partitioning has been used on a drive, you can use Disk Management. Right-click the disk, select Properties, and then select the Volumes tab—the partition style will be displayed. The same information can be gained using DiskPart.exe, by selecting the desired volume and using the LIST DISK command.

Partitioning and Multi-boot Scenarios

The limitations of MBR allow us only to create four partitions on a disk, each being assigned a drive letter. The first partition, the *primary*, which can be marked as "active," tells the BIOS which partition should contain the Windows system files that are required to boot from. If the active partition also contains the operating system files, it is also referred to as the *boot partition*.

In Windows, one of the primary partitions (not the boot partition) can then be used to create an extended partition. Within this special partition, you can create a further 23 drives, known as logical drives, each one with its own drive letter.

Dual booting was very common during the Windows XP era and again when Windows 7 was released. At that time, there was only one method of dual booting, which involved creating and dedicating a whole partition to the alternative operating system. This method was optimal for performance and allowed the full utility of all the system hardware resources; however, the disadvantage was that it reduced the amount of drive space available, because each operating system required its own discreet partition.

Modern dual-booting scenarios leverage the ability to boot to a VHD directly from the boot screen, so instead of booting to a physical partition, the PC is configured to see the virtual partition within the VHD and boot to this.

One step in advance of the legacy dual-boot and "boot to VHD" environments, the most common method of multi-booting your PC is to use Virtualization, such as Hyper-V, which is built into all Windows 8 and newer OS. Alternatives include VMware Workstation, VMware vSphere, Oracle VirtualBox, and Microsoft Virtual PC.

Booting to a VHD, or using a virtual machine, offers the user much more efficient space utilization, as virtual hard disks can be configured to dynamically expand, rather than being fixed. Performance-wise, hardware-based virtualization that uses hypervisor technologies offers excellent throughput for disk and network activity, compared to the pioneers of virtualization technology, which used software-based emulation providing suboptimal performance.

Windows File System Drivers

For Windows to interoperate with a specific file system, it requires a low-level driver. Windows supports many file systems, but the majority are not commonly known and work behind the scenes. In this book, we will focus on the most common, modern, and emerging file systems and provide a comparison to legacy files systems, where appropriate.

To see a complete list of the file systems that are supported on your Windows machine, load the System Information viewer, as shown in Figure 2-2. Follow these steps:

1. Start the System Information viewer by typing Msinfo32 in the Start Screen.

2. Select System Drivers under Software Environment.

3. Sort the list of drivers by clicking the Type column.

4. View the drivers with the type attribute of SERVICE_FILE_SYSTEM_DRIVER.

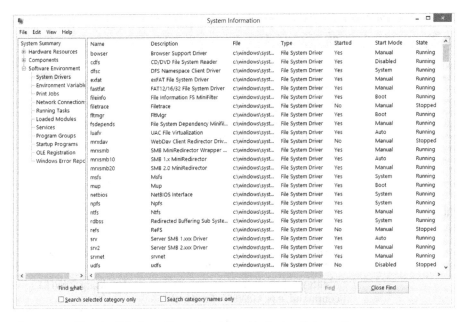

Figure 2-2. *Viewing Windows file system drivers in System Information*

FAT, FAT 32, and exFAT File Systems

Once you have created a partition, you are ready to format the volume so that Windows can create files and folders on the drive.

Windows supports many file systems, some which you may not encounter on a regular basis. These are CDFS, UDF, FAT12, FAT16, FAT32, exFAT, and NTFS. The most commonly used are NTFS and exFAT.

While some of these file systems have been in place for many years, we still rely on them for everyday use, such as when employing USB thumb drives that are formatted with a version of the FAT file system. For a brief overview of the FAT family of file systems, see Table 2-6.

Table 2-6. *File System Characteristics*

File System	Characteristics
FAT (FAT 16)	Introduced in 1981 and supported by DOS, OS/2, Linux, Windows 3.x and newer versions
	Volume size limit of 4GB
FAT 32	Supported by Windows 95 SP2 and newer versions; extended FAT 16 to allow larger number of files per partition
	File size limit of 4GB
	Volume size limit of 32GB

(continued)

Table 2-6. (*continued*)

File System	Characteristics
ExFAT (or FAT 64)	Extended file allocation table
	Supported on Vista SP1 and newer versions
	Designed by Microsoft specifically for flash storage devices
	Overcomes many of the limitations of earlier FAT versions while retaining widespread support
	Volume size limit of 256TB
	File size up to 16EB
	Supports more than 1000 files per directory
All versions of FAT, FAT32, exFAT	Widely supported
	No native file-level encryption or compression
	No local security for FAT or FAT32; anyone can read, change or delete any file stored on a FAT partition
	Ability to perform in-place conversion to NTFS using CONVERT command, e.g., CONVERT C: /fs:NTFS

■ **Note**   The FAT file system driver used by Windows is in the following location: %SystemRoot%\System32\Drivers\Fastfat.sys.

NTFS

The native file system used by Windows is NTFS (New Technology File System), and although it is significantly more complex than FAT, it offers sysadmins the ability to protect and secure the vast majority of files stored on enterprise servers throughout the world. Part of the design criteria for NTFS was that it must possess features to qualify as an enterprise-class file system.

In the following list includes some of the characteristics of NTFS in Windows:

- Introduced in Windows NT

- File-level compression

- Per-user volume quotas

- Symbolic links and junction points

- Volume sizes up to 256TB

- 2^{32}-1 files per volume

- Maximum file size in Windows NTFS of 16TB

- Enterprise-level file and folder encryption

- Recoverability by implementation of metadata transactional logging, to ensure file structure can be repaired

- Self-healing capabilities

The preceding list is not exhaustive but highlights the advanced capabilities offered by NTFS.

Hidden Gem: NTFS Symbolic Links

Application compatibility is a hot topic, owing to the need to upgrade to a modern operating system following the end of support for XP and Server 2003.

Many bespoke or custom written applications often have hard-coded file name paths that prevent them from working on a modern operating system (e.g., note the difference between C:\Program Files and C:\Program Files [x86]).

One of the hidden gems of NTFS, introduced in Windows Vista and newer versions, is the ability to create a symbolic link, which acts like a shortcut, thereby tricking the application into thinking it is directly accessing the desired file via the hard-coded path, when in reality it is being redirected to the file in a different path.

To experiment in your virtual lab environment, try the following command, logged on as an administrator, to demonstrate the power of a symbolic link:

1. Open an administrative command prompt.

2. Type C:\mklink demo.exe %windir%\system32\notepad.exe, then press enter.

3. Type demo.exe.

4. demo.exe launches Notepad via the symbolic link you have created.

5. Close Notepad.

6. In the command prompt, type DIR demo.exe.

7. Windows should display the <SYMLINK> identifier and display the path to the target file.

NTFS is a vast topic, and we will cover the permissions, encryption, ownership, and auditing features offered by NTFS in Chapter 3.

ReFS

You have seen earlier in the chapter that drive and partition technology has advanced over the years, and yet NTFS seems to have remained relatively static. NTFS has offered Windows users an enterprise class file system for nearly 20 years. During this time, there have been minor upgrades to NTFS and new capabilities added; however, the fundamental design has remained the same. This has been largely due to widespread adoption of NTFS and Microsoft's desire to maintain backward compatibility wherever possible.

Windows Server 2012 and Windows 8.1 were the first operating systems to offer support for a brand-new generation of Windows file system—the Resilient File System (ReFS). The need for a new file system has been driven by the advances in both hardware and software technologies that are fundamentally changing the way in which data is stored. Microsoft has stated that ReFS will be the file system that Windows will use during the next decade and beyond, as it will enable Windows to offer benefits to users in terms of storage stability, flexibility, scalability, and availability.

Listed are several of the recent trends in storage requirements that have prompted the emergence of ReFS, a modern file system that is not constrained by legacy compatibility needs.

- Data availability and "always on" demands

- Internet of Things (IoT) producing vast dataset sizes

- Enhanced data integrity for business-critical data

- Scalability and performance for dynamic workloads

■ **Note** ReFS is not intended to replace NTFS, at least not at the moment. Both file systems offer the sysadmin different capabilities.

Primarily, ReFS is relevant to server-based operations, and the most noticeable feature that has been optimized for ReFS is the new Storage Spaces, included in both Server 2012 and Windows 8, which brings new storage capabilities to organizations, offering high-availability, scalability, performance, and reliability at a very low cost. ReFS-aware Storage Spaces can automatically repair corrupt data and ensure that data is always available, even during drive failures.

ReFS offers enterprises support for data storage, with the characteristics shown in Table 2-7.

Table 2-7. *ReFS Characteristics*

Capability	Description
Transactional write model	Allows robust disk updating by multiple save points on disk, offering protection against power failures.
Proactive repairing/ self-healing	ReFS detects corruption and, when used in conjunction with Mirrored Storage Spaces, automatically repairs data that has been corrupted.
Improved data integrity	All metadata is check-summed to mitigate data and disk corruption.
Availability	ReFS volumes do not have to be taken offline to correct errors.
Scalability	ReFS works with extremely large datasets (PB and larger).

(*continued*)

Table 2-7. *(continued)*

Capability	Description
Application and backward compatibility	ReFS works with most NTFS features. Some features, however, are not supported, such as disk quotas.
Interoperability and flexibility	As a Microsoft component, ReFS can be integrated into the Windows storage model and are compatible with built-in and third- party low-level file-reliant software, such as backup and antivirus.

Limitations of ReFS

You should view ReFS as one tool in your file system toolbox. At present, there are some significant limitations to ReFS, listed below:

- Windows boot volume cannot be used with ReFS.

- ReFS does not support data reduplication.

- There is no support for disk quotas, encryption, and compression.

- ReFS is not supported on operating systems prior to Windows 8.1/ Windows Server 2012 nor on removable drives.

Future versions of Windows (Server and Client) may add capabilities to the ReFS file system, and the underlying storage stack, for example, Windows Server 2012 R2 added support for Clustered Shared Volumes (CSVs) and data tiering to Storage Spaces, which is a key "better together" partner of ReFS.

File System Tools and Utilities
ChkDsk

Although there were earlier versions of the Check Disk (ChkDsk) tool, in Windows 8 and later, it has been updated to work with such enhancements as the new self-healing capabilities of NTFS. Unless you are using Storage Spaces or some other form of data protection software, you have a proven backup in the event your data is at risk.

At the first indication that your disk is becoming error-prone and exhibiting behavior such as corrupt files or excessive thrashing, you should reach for the built-in Check Disk tool (ChkDsk.exe). Once you have run this tool, I would very much recommend that you review your backup regime, as more disk errors tend to eventual failure.

It is a small consolation that with SATA disks (and older types), due to the mechanical nature of their operation, we are normally given some notice of impending drive failure, through file corruption and other errors. However, most SSD drives fail suddenly and provide the user little or no warning whatsoever.

The ChkDsk.exe tool can be used to check for and repair issues found on FAT, FAT32, exFAT, and NTFS volumes. If you are running Windows 8 or later versions, ChkDsk will be able to repair most issues while the volume is still online. Most issues that are found on the boot and system drive will require the drive to be offline, which will require the tool to automatically carry out the repairs at the next system restart (though this can be postponed).

■ **Note** After successfully identifying a bad area or sector on a volume, the file system marks it as "bad" and hides it from the operating system, so that bad areas are never used again for data storage.

By default, Windows creates an automated scheduled task to run a volume health scan at 3 a.m., as part of the maintenance cycle. This task will only start if the device is connected to the AC supply; otherwise, it will carry forward until the next idle period when the device is connected.

To run the check, an NTFS drive manually carries out the following tasks in an administrative command prompt, as shown in Figure 2-3.

```
chkdsk /scan C:
```

Figure 2-3. Performing ChkDsk from the administrative command prompt

If errors are reported, you should attempt to repair the errors by using the following command:

```
chkdsk /spotfix C:
```

If the drive is a boot or system volume, ChkDsk will request that the fix operation be performed at the next reboot, as shown in Figure 2-4. The computer will restart automatically once complete.

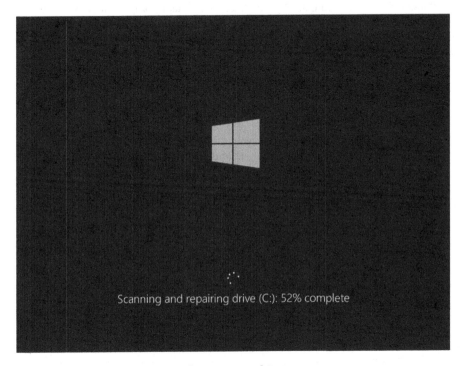

Figure 2-4. *ChkDsk scanning Windows 8 system drive*

If you are checking a volume formatted with a variety of the FAT file system, you should use the command: chkdsk C: and fix any issues reported with chkdsk c: /F.

■ **Note**   The ReFS system is self-healing and does not require checking with ChkDsk. If you attempt to run ChkDsk on an ReFS volume, you will receive the following response:

```
C:\Windows\system32>chkdsk /scan d:

The type of the file system is REFS.

The ReFS file system does not need to be checked.
```

Defragment

Files stored on traditional disks can become defragmented over time, due to the way in which Windows saves files to the next available space on a disk. Once a file is modified, it is typically not possible to save it back to the exact location again, and so part of the file is saved in the original location, but the other part is located elsewhere on the disk. This gives rise to the noncontiguous storage of files, otherwise known as defragmentation.

A very severely defragmented disk will suffer from slow disk performance, excessive disk thrashing, and a shortened life span.

Windows offers an automatically scheduled maintenance program for a system to self-defragment the drives. This is a scheduled task that should run weekly, and if the system is unable to run the Optimize Drives utility on three consecutive occasions, the user is notified via a pop-up message in the notification area and Action Center.

To start a manual defragmentation of your drives, as shown in Figure 2-5, take the following steps:

1. Type *defrag* into the Start screen and select **Defragment and optimize your drives**.

2. In the Optimize Drives utility, you can select the hard disk drive that you want to defragment and then click Optimize.

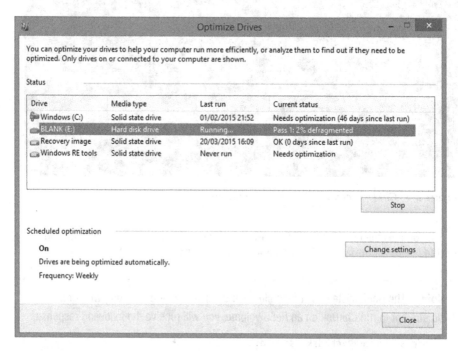

Figure 2-5. *Defragment your drives, using the Optimize Drives utility*

If you prefer to use the command line, you can open a command prompt and type *defrag* to use the Microsoft Drive Optimizer.

■ **Note**   SSD drives should not be defragmented. Files may become defragmented, but because files on the SSD are accessed at a uniform high speed regardless of the location or drive fragmentation, there is no need to optimize further. In fact, if a flash drive or SSD drive is defragmented, it can significantly reduce the life span of the drive.

CCleaner

In our book *Windows Registry Troubleshooting*, we introduced the popular CCleaner tool from Piriform as a great utility for cleaning up a system that has lots of temporary files, orphaned registry issues, and is generally a little unkempt. After running CCleaner, the system can then be defragmented, and it should operate more effectively after this maintenance.

Of course, you can also use the built-in Disk Cleanup tool, but we find the CCleaner tool faster and more optimal for cleaning a system. To use the Windows built-in cleanup tool, type *Clean* into the Start screen and select Disk Cleanup.

A file and registry cleaner will carry out some or all of the following activities:

- Scan your system for files left behind by application and uninstallers

- Remove unwanted/malicious entries to mitigate registry bloating

- Remove outdated or superseded temporary Internet files

- Remove incorrect file and program associations

- Restore the registry if any maintenance task fails

- Defragment the registry to remove any vacant spaces (empty placeholders left behind in the registry)

- Repair or remove system files, such as orphaned or shared DLL files, locate device drivers no longer required as well as old ActiveX files

- Schedule registry scans, ensuring that the registry is scanned and errors are repaired automatically

Many of the third-party cleaners available will remove excess bloat that every system can build up over time. It is recommended that you use this type of cleanup tool every few months.

Summary

On the face of it the Windows File System is a polished and functional part of Windows and especially for experienced users it has been built upon over many years and has become familiar quite familiar. As with all technology, there are new developments such as GPT disks, SSD drives and ReFS which are now supported by Windows and we need to understand how these technologies may be used.

One of the challenging parts of the Windows File System reveals itself in Chapter 3, as once we have configured our drives and formatted them as NTFS, we see how to troubleshoot file and folder permissions and access issues.

CHAPTER 3

■ ■ ■

Permissions, Ownership, and Auditing

Windows offers lots of very powerful features to prevent unauthorized access to your corporate data. The majority of these are available only when you use the New Technology File System (NTFS) that we reviewed in Chapter 2. In this chapter, we will delve further into the specifics of NTFS and focus on the features that allow you to secure your files by applying various permissions to accept or restrict access. We will provide you guidance on how to re-take ownership to gain control of orphaned files and, finally, review options for low-level fine-grained auditing of files and folders that are useful when investigating whether users are accessing (or attempting to access!) restricted files.

Throughout this chapter and the next on file security, we will highlight areas where it is all too easy to lock yourself out of a file or folder and ensure that you don't leave any back doors open!

Using the File System

- Configure File and Folder Permissions

- Review Effective Permission Issues

- Taking Ownership

- Configuring Auditing

- Tools

© Mike Halsey and Andrew Bettany 2015
M. Halsey and A. Bettany, *Windows File System Troubleshooting*,
DOI 10.1007/978-1-4842-1016-1_3

Configure File and Folder Permissions

You saw in the previous chapter that only volumes that are formatted with NTFS are able to set and apply NTFS file and folder permissions in Windows. Nearly every corporate network across the world incorporates NTFS file- and folder-level permissions, and the technology is robust, reliable, and effective.

As a sysadmin for a company or work group, you need to fully appreciate how to secure your environment, so that there is no unauthorized access to your corporate data, either from external threats or, more likely, users within the network.

Have you ever lost your home, car, or work office key or been locked out of somewhere? It is frustrating and can also be very embarrassing. In order to minimize the risk of becoming locked out of your own work or, worse, allowing unauthorized access to protected areas, we fully recommend that, while practicing the skills in this chapter, you work within a virtual lab environment and not on computers that are located on your production network.

It is also worth a reminder that throughout this chapter, you are most likely to be performing many actions using administrative-level privileges, and, therefore, you will be exempt from many of the built-in safeguards that Windows and NTFS enforces upon your non-admin colleagues. Effectively, you have a "master-key" to all the locks in the organization. Whenever you are setting permissions, you should always test to ensure that the outcome of your actions does not allow an unexpected increase of privilege for another user.

Review of ACLs, DACLs, and Permissions

Every PC has thousands of *objects*, the computer terminology for "something." An object can be just about anything, e.g., a file, a folder, or even a printer. With NTFS, we can set permissions on objects, so that we can control who gets access. In this section, we will explore how you can view and configure file and folder object permissions using either Windows Explorer (Windows 7 and earlier versions) or File Explorer (Windows 8 and newer versions), the command line, and Windows PowerShell. The list of permissions set on each object is called an Access Control List (ACL), and an example is displayed in Figure 3-1. This shows that the Accounting group has Modify (Allow), Read & execute (Allow), List folder contents (Allow), Read (Allow), and Write (Allow) permissions set for the Accounting folder.

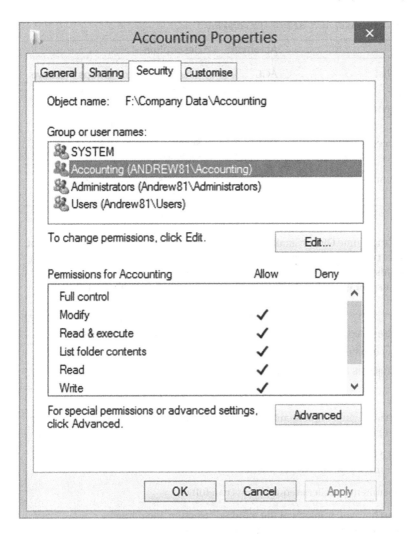

Figure 3-1. *Reviewing permissions for the Accounting folder*

While we are defining acronyms, we should also include ACE, DACLs, and SACLs for completeness. A description of each is shown in Table 3-1.

Table 3-1. *Descriptions of ACL, ACE, DACL, and SACL*

Name	Acronym	Description
Access control list	ACL	A list of users and groups that have permissions on the object
Access control entry	ACE	Identifies the specific permissions granted to a user or group
Discretionary access control list	DACL	Specifies who has what access to the object
System access control list	SACL	Specifies which operations are allowed by which users

For home and Home Office/Small Office (SOHO) users, the default permissions that are created on an object are normally sufficient for most needs. Within a larger corporate environment, this is seldom the case, and often quite elaborate schemes are put in place to ensure each user or group has the correct access to the objects within its jurisdiction.

■ **Tip** If you are faced with implementing NTFS permissions for a new project, ensure to allocate plenty of time to carry out the task—often the NTFS permissions aspect of an infrastructure project is afforded too little time.

As an overview, when implementing an NTFS permission strategy, you need to take the following steps:

1. Set a client meeting to understand the current user roles, groups, and access requirements.

2. Document the client requirements carefully.

3. Plan how you implement the required structure, including removing obsolete groups or adding any new ones, as necessary.

4. Build the structure in a controlled lab environment.

5. Thoroughly test the structure, using dummy files and review.

6. Implement the structure and migrate data.

7. Document the new structure and deliver it to the client.

Within NTFS, there are six basic and thirteen advanced permissions. The six basic permissions that can be assigned to a file or a folder are listed in Table 3-2.

Table 3-2. *Basic NTFS File and Folder Permissions*

Basic Permission	Description: When Applied to a Folder	Description: When Applied to a File
Full control	Allows the reading, writing, changing, and deletion of files and sub-folders. Allows modification of permissions on folders	Permits reading, writing, changing, and deletion of the file. Allows modification of permissions on files
Modify	Allows the reading, writing, changing, and deletion of files and sub-folders. Does not allow the modification of permissions on folders	Permits reading, writing, changing, and deletion of the file. Does not allow the modification of permissions on files
Read & execute	Allows the content of the folder to be accessed and executed	Allows the file to be accessed and executed
List folder contents	Allows the contents of the folder to be viewed	Cannot be applied to files
Read	Allows content to be accessed	Allows the contents to be accessed. Differs from Read & execute in that it does not allow files to be executed
Write	Allows adding of files and sub-folders	Allows a user to modify, but not delete, a file

■ **Note** Since Windows 8, the name of the standard permissions has been modified in the graphical user interface (GUI) to basic permissions, and special permissions have been changed to advanced permissions. Confusingly, Figure 3-1 still refers to the permissions as special permissions, although they are referred to as advanced permissions when you are editing the actual permission entries.

Whenever you set a top-level permission, such as Full control, Modify, or Read & execute, you will find that several other permissions are included as well. This behavior can be seen in Table 3-3.

Table 3-3. *Permissions Included When Setting Basic Permissions*

Basic Permission	Additional Permissions Included
Full control	Full control, Modify, Read & execute, List folder contents, Read, Write
Modify	Modify, Read & execute, List folder contents, Read, Write
Read & execute	Read & execute, List folder contents, Read
List folder contents	List folder contents
Read	Read
Write	Write

Should you not want to include these permissions, you will have to manually remove them before clicking Apply.

■ **Note**   It is not advisable to deviate from the basic permissions and their included default settings until you are proficient at setting advanced permissions.

Hidden from normal view is the matrix of advanced permissions that can also be applied to files and folders. It is worthwhile to take a look at how the basic permissions are actually collections of the 13 advanced permissions. The matrix in Table 3-4 shows the relationship between the basic and advanced permissions.

Table 3-4. *Relationship Between Basic and Advanced Permissions*

Advanced Permission	Full Control	Modify	Read & Execute	List Folder Contents	Read	Write
Traverse folder/ execute file	X	X	X	X		
List folder/read data	X	X	X	X	X	
Read attributes	X	X	X	X	X	
Read extended attributes	X	X	X	X	X	
Create files/write data	X	X				X

(*continued*)

Table 3-4. (*continued*)

Advanced Permission	Full Control	Modify	Read & Execute	List Folder Contents	Read	Write
Create folders/ append data	X	X				X
Write attributes	X	X				X
Write extended attributes	X	X				X
Delete sub-folders and files	X					
Delete	X	X				
Read permissions	X	X	X	X	X	X
Change permissions	X					
Take ownership	X					

When troubleshooting file and folder permissions, it is essential that you check to see if any advanced permissions have been set in error. Because the default basic permission screen does not show whether the advanced permissions are configured unless you scroll down below the Write permission, it is very easy to overlook these settings.

■ **Note**   The Delete permission is only available to holders of the Full control or Modify basic permissions. Similarly, only groups or users with Full control can modify file permissions.

Administrators are often thought of as "all powerful." Because they can utilize the Take Ownership right, they effectively have Full control over most objects and, therefore, can make modifications to file permissions.

When reviewing the ACLs, we can see that some permissions are grayed out, but others are not. This is because some permissions are explicitly set, while others are implied or inherited by virtue of their child relationship to a parent folder. We will cover inheritance in more detail next.

NTFS permission can take the form of various types, as shown in Table 3-5.

Table 3-5. Allowing and Denying NTFS Permissions

Permission Type	Description	Check Box Status
Explicit Allow	The user is allowed the permission on the object.	Check box is ticked.
Explicit Deny	The user is denied the permission on the object.	Check box is ticked.
Not configured	Permissions that have not been assigned have the effect of not allowing the user permission on the object.	Check box is clear.
Inherited Allow	Allow permission is applied to the object by virtue of permissions given to their parent object.	Check box is dimmed but checked.
Inherited Deny	Deny permission is applied to the object by virtue of permissions given to their parent object.	Check box is dimmed but checked.

Administrators who must script permissions have two choices: they can either use the command-line utility `icacls` or PowerShell, which is discussed later in this chapter.

The `icacls` utility allows users to configure and view permissions on NTFS objects on a local computer.

To grant a permission, the `/grant` switch is used, as shown in the following example, which grants Tommy the Modify permission to the F:\Company Data\Accounting\Payroll folder.

```
Icacls.exe F:\Company Data\Accounting\Payroll /grant Tommy:(OI)M
```

To deny a permission, the `/deny` switch is used, as shown in the following example, which denies Andrew the Read & execute permission to the F:\Company Data\Management folder.

```
Icacls.exe F:\Company Data\Management /deny Andrew:(OI)RX
```

■ **Note**   The (OI) refers to the inheritance flags of a permission and is used in the preceding example to apply the setting to files in this folder and in sub-folders.

For more information about the usage of icacls, take a look at the TechNet document at https://technet.microsoft.com/en-us/library/cc753525.aspx.

For even more flexibility, there are two PowerShell cmdlets that allow you to manage file and folder (any object) permissions, as shown in Figure 3-2. The two main cmdlets are Get-Acl and Set-Acl.

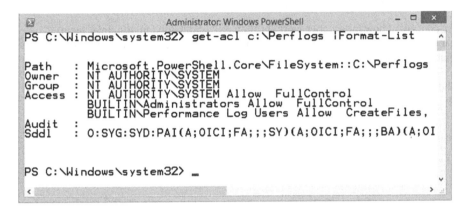

Figure 3-2. *Using PowerShell to view folder permissions*

For more information about the Get-Acl cmdlet, type Get-Help Get-Acl, or for information about the Set-Acl cmdlet, type Get-Help Set-Acl.

■ **Note** When troubleshooting permissions, do not always assume that Deny is consistently triumphant. While Explicit Deny will always take precedence when compared to other permissions, an Explicit Allow will trump an Inherited Deny.

Dynamic Access Control

In an Active Directory domain-based environment, you may also come across a feature available in Windows Server 2012 and Windows 8.1 called Dynamic Access Control (DAC). Rarely have I seen it deployed, except within legal or governmental establishments, but if your organization is looking for a robust way to apply data governance across your file servers to control and audit data access, DAC could work for you. DAC provides administrators the ability to set dynamic access controls on files and folders based on conditions that you can pre-configure within your Active Directory. The process is not enabled by default on the client side, but you can configure it by enabling the following Group Policy Object: Computer Configuration\Policies\Administrative Templates\System\KDC.

For more information on the steps required to configure DAC, see the following TechNet article "Introducing Dynamic Access Control": http://social.technet. microsoft.com/wiki/contents/articles/14269.introducing-dynamic-access-control.aspx.

Understanding NTFS Inheritance

The concept of how inheritance works is often well understood in principle, yet in practice, it still remains the cause of many permission-based blunders encountered when troubleshooting NTFS configurations.

In Figure 3-3, you can see in the "Inherited from" column from where any inheritance has been obtained. If there was no inheritance, the column indicates "None."

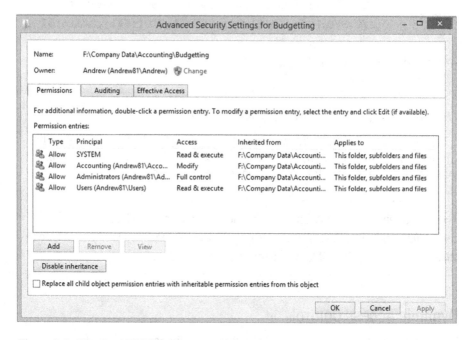

Figure 3-3. *Viewing NTFS Inheritance settings*

NTFS offers the ability to disable inheritance from taking place via a parent folder. When you click the Disable inheritance button shown in Figure 3-3, you will be offered the options shown in Figure 3-4.

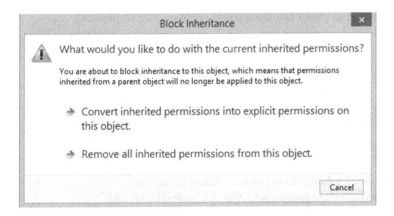

Figure 3-4. *Block Inheritance options*

There are three possible outcomes to this dialog box, with the easiest being Cancel, especially if you are not sure of the implications of selecting the other two choices. Table 3-6 offers a detailed description of each available option.

Table 3-6. *Options for Disabling Inheritance*

Option	Description
Convert inherited permissions into explicit permissions on this object	Instead of allowing inheritance to "flow" from top folders to the sub-folders, the "would be" inherited permissions are changed by the system from implicit permissions to explicit permissions. This could result in hundreds or thousands of inherited permissions being changed into explicit permissions.
Remove all inherited permissions from this object	This option completely removes all permissions and gives you a folder structure with no permissions at all. Be very careful if you choose to use this option, as it is extremely easy to forget to add back the SYSTEM account, which could cause complications for any system actions that expect to have SYSTEM access.

To disable NTFS inheritance, take the following steps on your Windows 8.1 computer:

1. Log on with an administrator account and open File Explorer.

2. Select the folder on which inheritance is to be disabled.

3. Right-click the folder and click Properties.

4. Click the Security tab and then select Advanced.

5. In the Permissions tab of the Advanced Security Settings dialog box, click Disable inheritance.

6. In the Block Inheritance dialog box, choose the option which you want to apply: click either the "Convert inherited permissions into explicit permissions on this object" option or click "Remove all inherited permissions from this object."

7. Click OK twice.

The most common error that an inexperienced sysadmin makes is to fail to draw a detailed schematic of how he/she wants the NTFS permissions to be applied to predefined users and groups. Typically, he/she will draw out a quick sketch of the desired outcome, begin creating the folder tree structure, and then apply permissions to this structure.

You should remember that inheritance should be used wherever possible, to ease administration. By default, all newly created folders will inherit permissions directly from the folder that they were created in. It is, therefore, essential that prior to building out the full folder structure, you first set up the outline structure, modify or remove the default inheritance, and then proceed to lay down the remainder.

Finally, our folder structure should not be created to mirror our organizational organigram—it should be laid out so that the folders and sub-folders work in favor of the IT administration staff, in the most logical and least administrative-intensive effort when setting and managing permissions.

Create a minimal folder structure first and then remove inheritance (option 1) initially. Configure the top-level permissions required for each uppermost folder and then re-enable inheritance for all child objects, by selecting the Replace all child permission entries with inheritable permission entries from this object option, as illustrated in Figure 3-5.

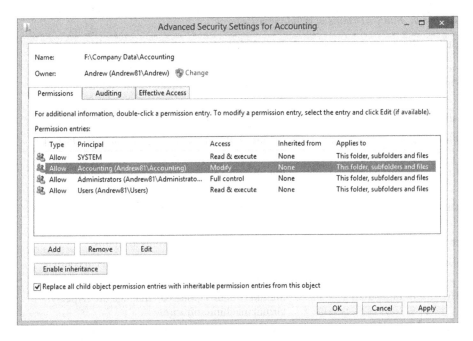

Figure 3-5. *Re-enabling child object inheritance*

Built-in Groups

When troubleshooting NTFS permissions, you may come across ACLs that do not contain any built-in groups, such as administrators or IIS_IUSRS. This is quite common; however, it is also a little disturbing.

Built-in groups are extremely valuable to the smooth running of Windows, and great care should be taken prior to removing any that may be included in an ACL.

You can find the list of the built-in groups on your computer by opening Computer Management and selecting Local Users and Group. There are 18 built-in groups, and they are listed in Table 3-7.

Table 3-7. *Built-in Groups in Windows 8.1*

Built-in Group	Description
Access Control Assistance Operators	Members can audit security settings to ensure that computers comply with an organization's security requirements.
Administrators	Members can do nearly anything on a computer.
Backup Operators	Members of this group can perform backups on a computer.
Cryptographic Operators	Members of this group can create certificates and perform other cryptography-related tasks.
Distributed COM Users	Legacy group—not really used, due to COM security vulnerabilities.
Event Log Readers	Members can monitor events log items.
Guests	Legacy group. The member Guest user account is disabled by default.
Hyper-V Administrators	Members of this group can manage the Hyper-V virtual machine software.
IIS_IUSRS	A System group used only to run Internet Information Services.
Network Configuration Operators	This group has privileges to configure network settings.
Performance Log Users	Members of this group can monitor performance logs.
Performance Monitor Users	Members can access performance counter data.
Power Users	Legacy group for backward compatibility.
Remote Desktop Users	Members have the right to log on across the network by using Remote Desktop.
Remote Management Users	Members can run network management tools to monitor and configure remote computers.
Replicator	Built-in service account to replicate files in a domain.
Users	Members include all users on the computer.
WinRMRemoteWMIUsers	Members can access WMI resources.

Built-in Service Accounts

In an ACL, you will see service accounts listed from time to time. The question often asked is whether these entries should be removed or retained? In the vast majority of cases, you should leave them intact. Whenever the local system account entries are removed, this invariably creates complications, as the system expects to have access to all resources.

The memberships that each system and service account provides are listed in Table 3-8. It is worth understanding that the local system account is even more powerful than a local administrator! The account allows the core Windows user-mode operating system processes to run, such as Session Manager (Smss.exe), Windows subsystem process (Csrss.exe), Local Security Authority (Lsass.exe), and the Logon process (Winlogon.exe).

Table 3-8. *Service Account Group Membership*

Local System (SYSTEM)	Network Service	Local Service
Everyone	Everyone	Everyone
Authenticated Users	Authenticated Users	Authenticated Users
Administrators	Users	Users
	Local	Local
	Network Service	Local Service
	Service	Service

When users remove inheritance from a folder or file, they sometimes remove all existing permissions, including any default system entries. These entries should be restored!

Moving or Copying Files and Folders

When you move or copy a folder from one location to another, you must be mindful of how Windows will perform the task with respect to file and folder permissions.

In the previous example, once you designed and set up your folder structure and NTFS permissions, you wouldn't want to lose all of those permissions because of how NTFS works across different locations.

In Table 3-9, we highlight the behavior that NTFS exhibits when copying files from one folder to another folder and also between partitions.

Table 3-9. *Effect of Moving or Copying NTFS Files*

Action	Effect
Copy or Move a file or folder to a *different* partition	Inherits the permissions from the destination (new location) folder
Copy or Move a file or folder within the *same* NTFS partition	Inherits the permissions from the new parent folder, and explicitly assigned permissions are retained and merged with those inherited

Copying a file or folder from NTFS to a non-NTFS partition such as a FAT partition will result in all NTFS file and folder permissions being lost. As you have seen earlier, only users with the Full control permission (and administrators) are able to perform this task, because it changes the permissions of the files and folders.

Effective Access

Sometimes, when several layers of permissions, both explicit and inherited and with membership of several groups, are applied to an object, it can be challenging to calculate the permissions that would affect a particular user or group.

NTFS provides the Effective Access feature (previously called Effective Permissions) that will easily allow one to determine the effective permission a user or group has on any object, as shown in Figure 3-6. It is essential when setting permissions in a corporate environment that NTFS permissions are verified, to ensure that the expected results are as desired. The Effective Access feature is located on the Effective Access tab of the Advanced Security Settings of each object.

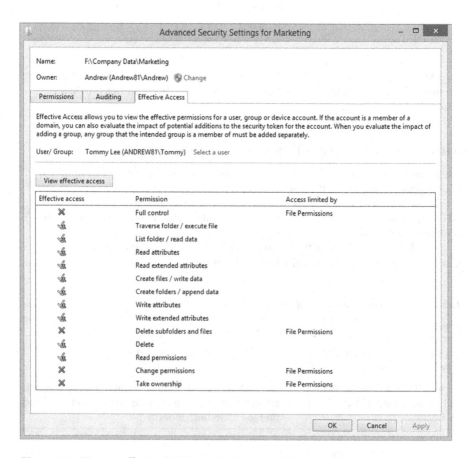

Figure 3-6. *Viewing effective NTFS permissions on a folder*

■ **Note**   The Effective Access tool will not take into account those permissions given to a user if he/she is also the Creator Owner of the object.

■ **Troubleshooting Tip**   When you are troubleshooting NTFS permission issues relating to a specific user or group, it is useful to review the effective permissions on that user.

Taking Ownership

Have you ever attached an old hard drive to your system only to become frustrated that you cannot access any of the files or folders on the drive? The reason why you cannot access those files is because you don't have the necessary permission. Thankfully, NTFS has a feature that allows you (normally with your administrator hat on) to add a new "owner" to the permissions of the file. Some organizations utilize disk or file quotas that can restrict the data volume that a user can create. Users are often quite unaware that quotas are in existence. Because quotas are applied based on file ownership if they are set to be too restrictive, problems can arise when users attempt to create new files that then exceed the quota limit. The file system will prevent further files being created, unless an administrator increases the quota size, or the size of the data owned by the user is reduced (by deleting files).

If the user can still access his/her files and folders, then he/she can also "give away" ownership of the resources to another user. This can be particularly useful if a temporary member of staff has been creating documents, and he/she has to hand over the documents at the end of an assignment. More often, this never happens, and in practice, the administrator is required to reassign ownership once the matter becomes a problem!

To change the owner of a file or folder, click the Change link on the Advanced Security Settings dialog box for the file or folder that you want to modify, then select the new owner, as shown in Figure 3-7.

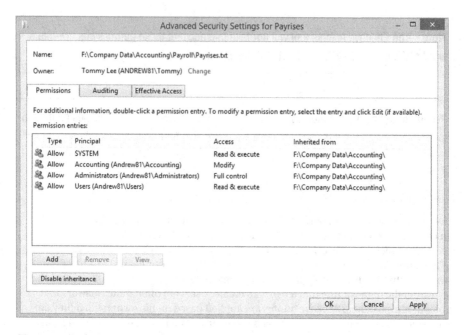

Figure 3-7. *Changing ownership on a file or folder*

Auditing

The term *auditing* makes me think of accounting—numbers, checks, and balances. In a workplace, nearly everything has a specific role, everyone has an ID, and each user is given access only to the areas that he/she needs. The ramifications of the Sarbanes-Oxley Act (2002) created a whole new level of checks and balances that managements are now requiring, to ensure that everything in the business is accounted for and that access is tightly controlled. Auditing is an in-depth defensive tool that is normally the last line of defense.

To ensure that we have defense in depth, we should take a multilayered approach to protecting our data. One example of layering could be as follows:

1. Set the security on the disk using BitLocker (see Chapter 5).

2. Set permissions on the folders and files.

3. Set auditing to watch the folders and files.

Ultimately, you should not rely solely on one method of protection. If you simply set the NTFS permissions and then leave them alone, you are only relying on NTFS to protect the folders and files. Should a change occur that circumvents the NTFS permissions, such as a junior admin makes a group change and gives a user more privileges than before, the protection could be breached. Auditing would alert you at a very early stage of the vulnerability and allow you to rectify the situation before it became more damaging to the corporation (and, potentially, your career).

While we are focused in this chapter about files and folders, the Windows Auditing feature is much more powerful than simply being able to audit objects. It can record the following:

- Successful logons

- Unsuccessful logons

- Changes to accounts in Active Directory

- Who has accessed or tried to access files

- Who has modified or deleted files

- Who has used objects, such as printer devices

- Who restarted a system

The list of actions that can be audited is not exhaustive, and the recording also includes data such as the date, time, user account, location, and file name.

Auditing must be enabled on the system via the Group Policy or the local security policy (Security Settings\Local Policies\Audit Policy), as shown in Figure 3-8. Once it is enabled, you then configure what you want to audit. This is done on the actual object, such as the folder that contains sensitive documents.

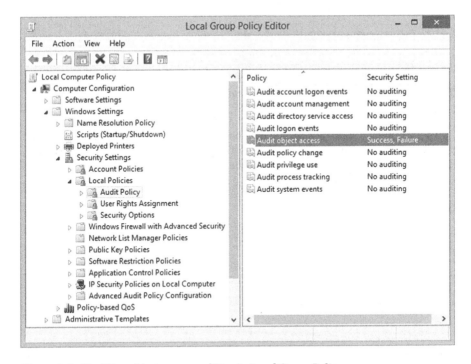

Figure 3-8. Enabling object access auditing in Local Group Policy

As shown in Figure 3-9, you should take care to specify auditing on specific activities, such as whether a user or group can Read, Modify, or Delete the file(s); otherwise, the amount of logging will be extensive. Auditing allows a very granular level of recording to take place, which can be intensive for the system if over-provisioned.

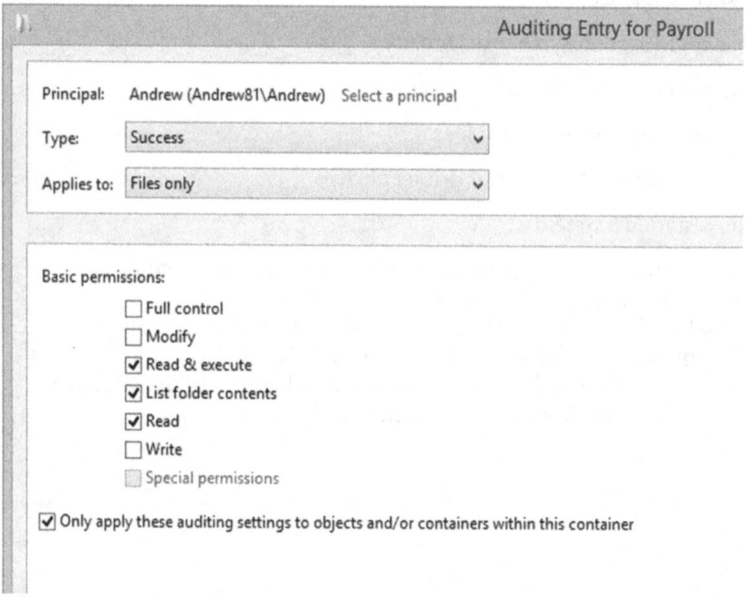

Figure 3-9. Configure auditing criteria on a folder

After you enable audit logging, you then have to open the Event Viewer Security log to view the audited events. You will notice from Figure 3-10 that simply opening a single file within a monitored area will generate dozens of log entries.

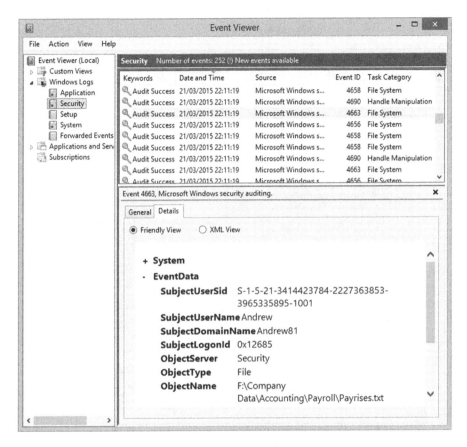

Figure 3-10. *Viewing auditing events in the Security Log*

The event viewer is a powerful tool, and you could configure a task to be performed whenever a specific event takes place. To enable this, you would set up auditing in your lab environment, review the security log entries, and identify the events that are triggered when an intruder or unauthorized user accesses the folder or files under scrutiny.

Once you have identified the log entry that corresponds to the event you are interested in, you would select Attach Task To This Event... from the Action pane within Event Viewer. You can then attach a PowerShell script that alerts you. In Windows 7, you were able to create an e-mail alert whenever a specific event was triggered, but this component has been deprecated.

If you need to modify a task that is created, you would have to edit the task within the Task Scheduler, as indicated in Figure 3-11.

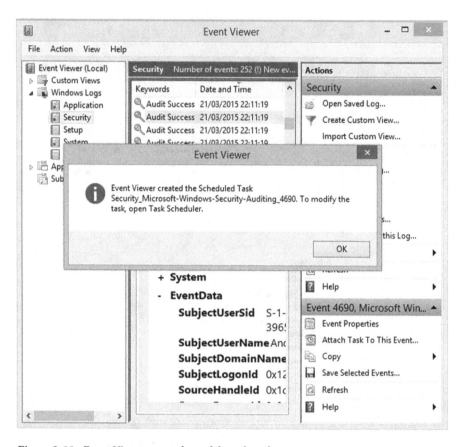

Figure 3-11. *Event Viewer created a task based on the event*

■ **Troubleshooting Tip** When testing auditing, you may have to log off the system and log on again with the correct test user account.

Tools

We have seen that when copying or moving files that contain NTFS permissions, the permissions sometimes are lost, depending on the destination. To overcome this undesired behavior, you can use built-in tools: Xcopy, Robocopy.exe, or icacls.exe.

These tools will move files from one volume to any NTFS destination volume, while retaining their existing permissions.

Xcopy is a legacy tool and offers fewer features than Robocopy, and because we have already introduced `icacls` earlier in the chapter, I will focus on Robocopy.

Previously found only in the Windows Resource Kit, it has been made even more popular, as rather than being a separate download, Robocopy (Robust File Copy for Windows) is now included with Windows 7 and newer versions of Windows. The bundled version now also includes a multi-threading feature allowing users to specify the number of threads that the tool can work with, thus allowing the tool to process multiple streams of data simultaneously.

The main features of Robocopy, after speed, are the ability to preserve extended attributes, backup capabilities, and restart ability.

All of the available options can be seen by typing "Robocopy /?" at the command prompt or PowerShell interface, as shown in Figure 3-12.

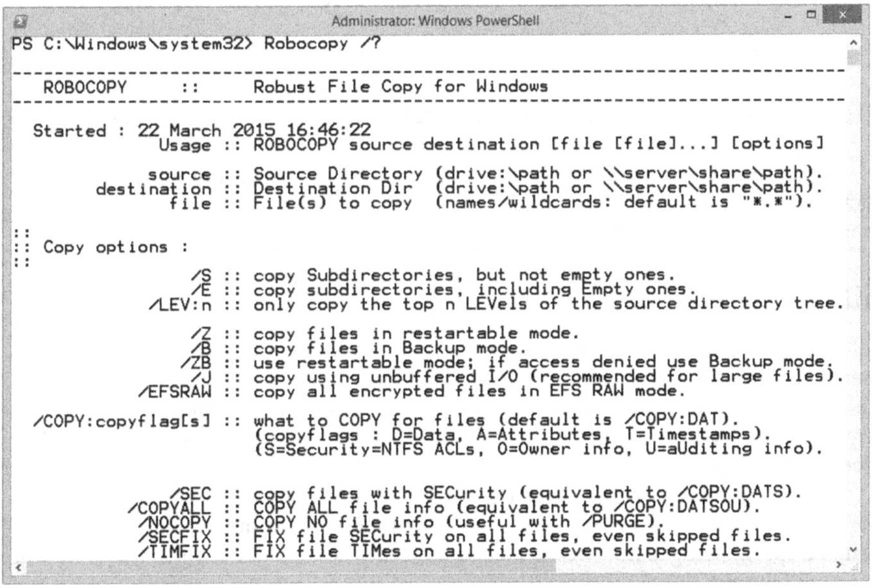

Figure 3-12. Robocopy switches in a PowerShell command line

For example, if you wanted to move F:\Company Data\Accounting\Payroll to the folder G:\Confidential Data with all the data and retain share and security permissions, you would use the following command:

```
Robocopy.exe F:\Company Data\Accounting\Payroll G:\Confidential Data /S /
COPY:DATS
```

Other nice features of Robocopy are that it is

- Very fast and reliable
- Easier to script (though you should use PowerShell in preference to Robocopy, if you are seeking powerful scripting abilities)
- Re-tries when errors occur
- Copies over more file attributes than Xcopy

Finally, if you are not a command-line junkie and prefer the GUI, you could try the following GUI versions of Robocopy:

Robocopy GUI

`https://technet.microsoft.com/en-gb/magazine/2006.11.utilityspotlight.aspx`

RichCopy

`https://technet.microsoft.com/en-gb/magazine/2009.04.utilityspotlight.aspx`

Both of these tools are available via TechNet Magazine and are not supported by Microsoft.

Summary

Delving in the Windows NTFS permissions can be a daunting task and when faced with needing to troubleshoot access issues it becomes vitally important that you understand the relationships, rules and consequences of clicking "apply", especially if we are logged in as an administrator. It is however a core skill for IT pro and enthusiast to master and become confident.

Once you have fully grasped the differences between Deny and Allow and understand when you would use `icacls` you should be ready to build your knowledge further by progressing to how we are able to share files across our networks which we will cover in Chapter 4.

CHAPTER 4

■ ■ ■

Managing File Sharing

In the last chapter, we explored many of the features that New Technology File System (NTFS) provides to secure files and folders from a local environment. The most common (and easiest) type of unauthorized attack seeks to gain access directly to a computer on the network from within an office. With the knowledge and tips gained from the last chapter, your local files should be relatively safe. However, we will now explore the possibility that the intruder has managed to infiltrate your network, or has hacked through your firewall, perhaps via a stolen laptop, and now is searching your network for any vulnerabilities.

This chapter will look at how Windows shares files. It will also discuss how you can ensure that files are secure when shared across the network and how to become aware of common back doors, such as administrative shares, offering simple ways to reduce your risk of compromise before revisiting some additional NTFS features that could not be squeezed into the last chapter!

Sharing Corporate Resources

When you need to share files and folders, you could use "legacy" methods, such as CDs, DVDs, and even thumb drives, but the most efficient and effective way is to use a network. Administrators often have to maintain a fine balance between convenience and security. All methods of storing corporate data on removable media pose a significant security risk. Vast amounts of personal, corporate, or even confidential government data stored on removable media is routinely lost in the mail, stolen, or even left behind on public transportation, only to reach the news headlines on a regular basis.

Storing data on a network can also be risky, but less so. The main difference between network storage and removable storage is that you, the sysadmin, have the ability to secure and protect the data against potential vulnerabilities. For an increasing number of businesses, the explosion of cloud storage offerings, such as OneDrive, Dropbox, Google Drive, and others, also provides huge convenience and cost savings, but for the majority of businesses, there are still many unanswered questions about these services, such as future costs, security, and reliability.

In this chapter, we are particularly interested in the ability to make our file resources available to our users over our own corporate network. Ever since Windows 3.11 for Workgroups, Microsoft has embraced network sharing, and it continues to improve the ease and scope of the networking features in Windows.

© Mike Halsey and Andrew Bettany 2015
M. Halsey and A. Bettany, *Windows File System Troubleshooting*,
DOI 10.1007/978-1-4842-1016-1_4

■ **Note** This book is aimed at the IT pro and enthusiast, therefore we will not provide detailed explanations of the consumer-focused networking features included in Windows, such as HomeGroup and Public Folder Sharing.

Sharing allows multiple users to access files from anywhere across the network. Depending on how you set up your networking infrastructure, your network could allow the file locations and types of connections shown in Table 4-1.

Table 4-1. *Types of Network Connections to Corporate Resources*

Type of Network	Description
Local network	Most common network with shared resources located on a file server
Intranet web site	Files hosted on a file server with access via internal corporate web server
SharePoint	Internal or externally hosted SharePoint (Intranet/Extranet) holding files within a SharePoint site
Virtual Private Network (VPN)	On demand method of connecting to a corporate network securely from a remote/external location via the Internet or dial-up
Direct Access	"Always on" method of connecting to corporate network securely from a remote/external location via the Internet

We discussed creating a logical hierarchy folder structure when designing your corporate resources and recommended that you use this approach for both NTFS security reasons and for ease of administrative maintenance.

We will cover in this section the following aspects of shared networking:

- How Windows Manages Shared Folders
- Enabling File Sharing
- Sharing Files and Folders
- Sharing Folders Using File Explorer
- Sharing Folders Using Computer Management
- Sharing Folders from the Command Line
- Combining Share Permissions and NTFS Permissions
- Access-Based Enumeration (ABE)

How Windows Manages Shared Folders

As you saw in Chapter 3, we use NTFS to manage file and folder permissions on a local computer. Shares are not managed by NTFS, but, rather, the majority of Windows-based network access is provided by Server Message Block (SMB). Share permissions and NTFS permissions are independent of each other, and neither changes the other. The access permissions on a shared folder are determined by taking into consideration both the share permission and the NTFS permissions. Whenever we create a shared folder, there will be share permissions (SMB), which can be even more restrictive than the NTFS permissions.

■ **Note** SMB permissions are not taken into account by Windows at all if the user accesses the resource locally or by logging on via Remote Desktop. For this reason, it is essential that NTFS permissions are properly configured independently.

The various different versions of SMB used by Windows operating systems are shown in Table 4-2. You can check the version that you are currently using by employing the PowerShell cmdlet Get-SmbConnection. Perform this cmdlet while you are connected remotely (via a SMB share) to a shared folder located on a file server. Windows automatically negotiates between the client and server to ensure that the same version is used whenever there is a potential for a disparity in versions.

Table 4-2. Windows-Supported Versions of SMB

Version	Supported by
SMB 1.0 (or SMB1)	Windows 2000, Windows XP, Windows Server 2003, and Windows Server 2003 R2
SMB 2.0 (or SMB2)	Windows Vista (SP1 or later) and Windows Server 2008
SMB 2.1 (or SMB2.1)	Windows 7 and Windows Server 2008 R2
SMB 3.0 (or SMB3)	Windows 8 and Windows Server 2012
SMB 3.02 (or SMB3)	Windows 8.1 and Windows Server 2012 R2

■ **Note** The change from SMB 2.0 to SMB 3.0 and 3.02 offers some significant advances in functionality to SMB. For more information on SMB for Windows, take a look at http://blogs.technet.com/b/josebda/archive/2013/10/02/windows-server-2012-r2-which-version-of-the-smb-protocol-smb-1-0-smb-2-0-smb-2-1-smb-3-0-or-smb-3-02-you-are-using.aspx.

Enabling File Sharing

You can create shared folders on a server or client computer. Because of the potential security risks exposed by allowing users the ability to access a computer via the network, Windows clients do not enable file sharing by default. Each computer needs to explicitly enable the ability to allow sharing, and this is done within the Network and Sharing Center, which is the centralized location for networking tasks. To turn on sharing, follow these steps:

1. Open Control Panel, select Network and Internet.

2. Choose Network and Sharing Center.

3. On the left, choose Change advanced sharing settings.

4. Windows will automatically expand the network profile in use, so you can change the setting quickly for the current network profile.
   Network profiles are: Private, Guest, or Public. All networks enable file and printer sharing by selecting Turn on file and printer sharing.

5. Click Save changes, as shown in Figure 4-1.

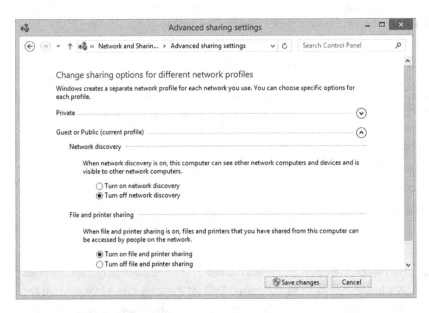

Figure 4-1. Enable file sharing

In a domain environment, this setting is also configurable by using Group Policy.

You may also notice in Figure 4-1 the ability to toggle network discovery on and off. This is a feature introduced in Windows Vista that utilizes a new protocol called Link Layer Topology Discovery (LLTD). Operating at the Layer 2 of the network, it allows Windows to identify with other devices on the local subnet and, additionally, evaluate bandwidth capabilities (QoS) of the network.

By enabling network discovery on your computer, you are relaxing the firewall security settings so that your computer will become "discoverable" on the network by other Windows clients, and your computer can see other network computers and devices.

Obviously, reducing the effectiveness of the firewall is a potential risk, and for this reason, network discovery is disabled by default. An organization can manage the status and settings of the LLTD Mapper (LLTDIO) and Responder (RSPNDR) via two Group Policy settings, which can be found here: Computer Configuration\Policies\ Administrative Templates\Network\Link Layer Topology Discovery.

Sharing Files and Folders

We may think that sharing a folder is a relatively trivial matter and that file servers will hold dozens or hundreds of shared folders. You must remember that each shared folder is a potential vulnerability, allowing access directly into and onto the corporate network. Only users who are members of the Administrators, Power Users, and Server Operators groups have the ability to universally create shared folders. This restriction is very effective in preventing shared folder sprawl. If you do need to allow other types of users, or perhaps a group, to have the ability to share folders (perhaps you have a team that needs to share a project folder hosted in an isolated file server), you should create a group and grant it the *Create Permanent Shared Objects* user right, which is found in Group Policy.

There are several tools that we can use to share files and folders, as listed following:

- Sharing Folders using File Explorer

- Sharing Folders using Computer Management MMC snap-in

- Sharing Folders from the Command Line: Net Share & PowerShell

When using Windows 8 in a work group scenario, a maximum of 20 concurrent users are allowed to access a shared resource. When using a file server to share files and folders, there is no maximum. However, unless you have specific requirements, it is best to leave the setting to default. If you decide to restrict the number of concurrent users based on your organizational needs, you should make this setting reasonable, as Windows will enforce this as a hard limit on a first-come, first-served basis. It is advisable to document the setting clearly, because if users complain at a future date about being unable to access files on the same file server, you may endure a long period of scratching your head, exploring reasons for the error, before you fall upon this obscure and rarely modified setting.

■ **Best Practice** When designing a folder structure, especially one that will be shared across the network, it is better to have a wide, rather than a deep, multilevel hierarchy of folders. This may appear counterintuitive at first glance, but wide structures are inherently more secure with inheritable permissions set at the highest level and allowed to flow. By using the ability to compartmentalize data in this way, you will reduce variations to the way NTFS permissions work (i.e., blocked inheritance), and this will reduce administrative burden and errors.

Sharing Folders Using File Explorer

To manually share a folder within File Explorer, you should right-click the folder that you want to share, click Properties, and then select the Sharing tab, as shown in Figure 4-2.

Figure 4-2. Individually sharing folders in File Explorer

You have two choices:

- **Share**—This uses Basic sharing (not recommended in a corporate environment). Simply click the Share button and follow the wizard to share the folder.

- **Advanced Sharing**—Traditional fine-grained folder sharing

The advanced sharing option allows you to

- Create the share name (which can be different from the actual folder name)

- Permit the fine-grained setting of share permissions

- Set caching of the folder, if you want to use offline files

The permissions ACL is shown in Figure 4-3, displaying the default permissions on a newly created share: Everyone: Allow Read.

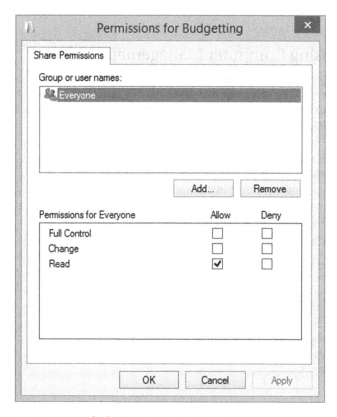

Figure 4-3. *Default Share Permissions ACL*

We can edit the share permissions, adding users and groups to which we want to give access. We will discuss the built-in Everyone group later in this chapter. Remember that share permissions have a huge impact on the overall level of permissions. A user or a group can never gain more permissions in addition to those granted by the share. When the NTFS and Share permissions are evaluated, the most **restrictive** of the permissions on either side are permitted. Where a user is a member of several groups and has different permissions based on his/her membership, his/her overall share permissions are cumulative.

You can stop sharing a folder at any time, by right-clicking the shared folder. Click Share with and then click Stop Sharing.

■ **Best Practice**   The default SMB share permission is Everyone: Allow Read only. This is very restrictive and not useful in most situations, and you should modify this. Best practice would modify this to *Specific Group*: Allow Full Control and then restrict access to the file and folder using NTFS permissions.

Sharing Folders Using Computer Management

You must have administrative privileges to create shares using the Computer Management MMC snap-in. A major advantage that Computer Management provides the administrator (subject to the remote system firewall allowing this) is the ability to create shared folders remotely, by connecting the MMC to another computer.

To create a shared folder using Computer Management, follow these steps:

1. Open Control Panel, click System and Security, click Administrative Tools, and then open Computer Management. (You can also use compmgmt.msc in the Start screen and then press Enter, or right-click the Start button and select Computer Management from the context menu.)

2. Expand System Tools\Shared Folders and select Shares.

3. To create a new share, right-click the Shares label and select New Share...

4. The Create A Shared Folder Wizard will launch, then click Next.

5. Enter the Folder path or click Browse to find the folder you want to share. You can also create a new folder to share, as shown in Figure 4-4.

6. Click Next.

7. Provide a share name and a description (optional).

8.   You can modify the offline settings if required.

9.   Click Next, to display the Shared Folder Permissions options, as shown in Table 4-3.

10. Choose the permissions that you require and click Finish twice.

■ **Note**   By default, Computer Management will connect to the local computer, but if you right-click the Computer Management (Local) label, you can select the Connect to another Computer option, to connect to a different device on your network.

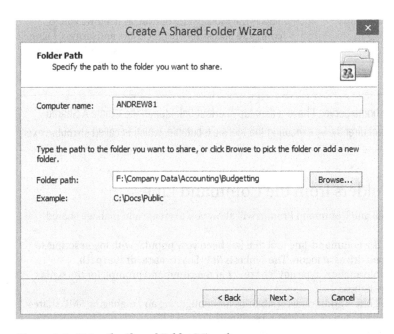

Figure 4-4. Using the Shared Folder Wizard

The permission options provided by the Shared Folder Wizard are described in Table 4-3.

Table 4-3. *Setting Shared Folder Permissions Within the Shared Folder Wizard*

Permission	Description
All Users Have Read-Only Access (Default)	Gives users the ability to view files and read data but not to create, modify, or delete files and folders
Administrators Have Full Access; Other Users Have Read-Only Access	Gives administrators full access to shared folders; other users have read-only access. Administrators can create, modify, and delete files and folders. Within NTFS, administrators have the right to change permissions and to take ownership of files and folders, while other users can only view files and read data
Administrators Have Full Access; Other Users Have No Access	Gives only administrators full access to the shared folder
Customize Permissions	This is the most useful option, as it allows you to configure access for specific users and groups, using the advanced ACL options for the share permissions.

■ **Tip**　On my home server, I have a desktop shortcut link launch the Create A Shared Folder Wizard tool directly, by executing the tool's executable, which is called `shrpubw.exe`.

Sharing Folders from the Command Line

Both PowerShell and Command Prompt will allow you to create and manage shared folders.

Net Share is a command-line tool that has been very popular with logon scripts to establish mapped drives at logon. The syntax is `Net Share name=drive:path`.

For more information, type `net share /?` at the command prompt, for the syntax and available switches.

PowerShell offers additional capabilities for configuring and managing SMB shares locally and remotely, which can also be scripted.

A sample SmbShare PowerShell command to create a new SMB share called AccountsShared, which shares the F:\Company_Data\Accounting folder, can be created by typing the following:

```
New-SmbShare –Name AccountsShared –Path F:\Company_Data\Accounting
```

The cmdlets available within the SmbShare module are

- `Block-SmbShareAccess`
- `Get-SmbShare`
- `Get-SmbShareAccess`

- `Grant-SmbShareAccess`

- `New-SmbShare`

- `Remove-SmbShare`

- `Revoke-SmbShareAccess`

- `Set-SmbShare`

- `Unblock-SmbShareAccess`

For more information, you can type `get-help smbshare` in a Windows PowerShell prompt.

Combining Share Permissions and NTFS Permissions

We learned in Chapter 3 that NTFS permissions on a file or folder will be set on the ACL, and these entries will determine the scope of access to the resource. This is true for local access, i.e., interactive logon sessions. Windows will evaluate the user credentials and grant or deny access to the resource. However, if the file or folder is accessed across the network, you have to consider additional constraints that may be imposed on the resource by the service providing the access.

Although it may sound obvious, it is worth stating: when you create a shared folder, the folder should already be present on the file server, and, most important, it is best practice that you have already configured the NTFS level permissions in advance of making the resource available as a shared folder. In this way, both types of permissions are set according to a predetermined plan, rather than using an ad-hoc security approach.

New administrators often make the mistake of using both share permissions (SMB) and NTFS permissions to secure folders and files. Share permissions do not secure files and folders. They only restrict the access to them via the network, and all share permissions can be bypassed by connecting locally. In nearly all cases, the permissions should be set at the NTFS level, and the share permission should be set to (Everyone: Allow Full Control). In my experience, I like to modify the starting point for a share permission slightly, to Authenticated Users: Allow Full Control. Of course, this could be tightened further by replacing Authenticated Users with the specific group that you want to access the resource.

▦ **Best Practice**   Faced with a situation in which you may have different teams or departments, each requiring access to the same folder, you can create multiple instances of the same share. For example, you may have a sales team that needs Read/Write access and the ability to use offline files and a marketing team that is required to have Modify permissions but cannot take the files offline. You can share the Sales & Marketing folder twice, each with a different name, and these are published to the departmental users. In this way, the underlying NTFS permissions are unchanged, but the SMB settings that relate to the share and the ability to take files offline enforce the requirements.

Just as with NTFS permission inheritance, the share permissions that apply to a shared folder will also apply to all files in that folder, to sub-folders, and to all files in those sub-folders when the content is being accessed through the share.

Sometimes I use the following analogy when explaining what happens when you combine NTFS and share permissions. If you think that the shared folder is the doorway allowing access to the files inside the network, you can then imagine that the share permissions you are handed as you pass through the front door are the most that you could ever achieve. So, if the shared folder permission is set to Read, the most that you ever hold is read, even if an individual NTFS file permission is set to Modify. The combined effect would be that you have Read access only via the network. Of course, you could ignore the front door and gain access through a hidden back door, thereby avoiding share permissions altogether. We will cover hidden shares later in this chapter.

■ **Troubleshooting Tip**   Are your shared folders no longer working after your junior admin has tidied them up? If the underlying folder that is shared using SMB is moved or renamed, the share permissions on those folders are lost.

Access-Based Enumeration (ABE)

Ever since Windows NT, one of the criticisms of Windows is that users are able to "see" shared files and folders on the file server. If users encounter a file or folder that they are not entitled to access, then NTFS permissions will control and restrict actual access to the object. Other operating systems, such as Novell NetWare, would only allow users to "see" the existence of resources that they had permission to access.

Some administrators seek to hide folders that are not relevant to users by careful folder hierarchy design and extensive permission management.

Access-based enumeration, which is included as a feature within the file server role since Windows Server 2008 (previously this was a separate download for Windows Server 2003 SP1, and, therefore, it was not widely deployed), allows sysadmins to correct this situation and forces Windows to evaluate each and every shared object, to ensure that resources are effectively hidden from users, unless they have at least the Read permission on the resource.

ABE can be utilized for the whole file server, or deployed only on specific file shares, though it is not enabled by default when you provision a new shared folder, as shown in Figure 4-5.

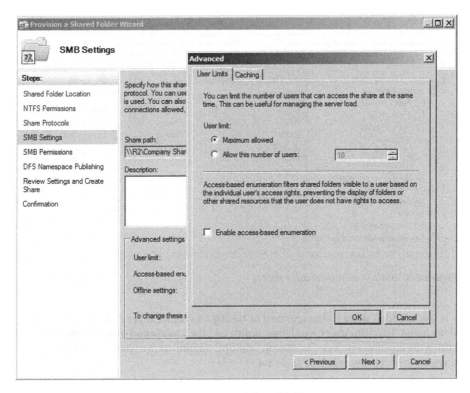

Figure 4-5. Configuring ABE on a server-based shared folder

■ **Note**   ABE only works for shared resources. If the user is able to access the resource locally or via Remote Desktop Connection, he/she would be accessing the resource directly, and ABE would be redundant. NTFS is always the primary protector on local resources.

Administrative and Hidden Shares

As administrator, you are given nearly all of the keys to most IT-related locks within your organization. We have learned about accessing folders and files across the network, using the published "public" shared folders. Windows has a built-in set of hidden shares that local and domain administrators can use to connect directly to any computer on the network—including servers.

The built-in administrative shares are shown in Figure 4-6 and can also be obtained by typing net share into a command prompt.

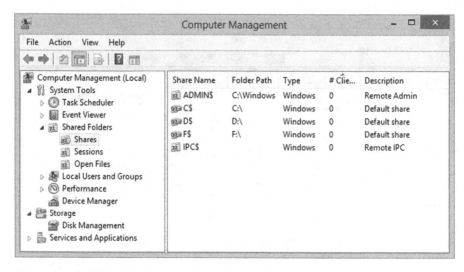

Figure 4-6. *Built-in administrative shares*

Each hidden share is characterized by having a $ symbol appended to the end of the share name. To create your own shares, simply add the $ to the end of the share name during the creation process. The default (built-in) administrative (sometimes called *special*) shares are described in Table 4-4.

Table 4-4. *Default Administrative Shares*

Share Name	Description
Drive$	Root directory of a drive, e.g., C$
ADMIN$	Remote administration. Pointing to C: \Windows
IPC$	A programming feature that lets processes communicate with one another using named pipes
NETLOGON	Active Directory domain environment to locate a domain controller in an Active Directory environment
SYSVOL	Required by domain controllers in an Active Directory environment to store Group Policy Objects (GPOs) and other scripts
PRINT$	Used for remote administration of printers
FAX$	Used for administration of fax clients

> ■ **Note** Marking a share name ending with $ as a hidden share and not showing it when accessing an SMB host from the network is only observed by Windows clients and Windows Servers. Linux clients will expose these "hidden" shares with ease.

> ■ **Troubleshooting Tip** You can remove the root directory administrative shares when not required and run a script to re-enable them during a planned maintenance cycle. You should never disable the SYSVOL or NETLOGON shares on Active Directory Domain Controllers. Finally, do not disable the other administrative shares, unless you are sure no tools or utilities require them to be present. You should also check on the network, to see if additional hidden shares have been created.

Security Identifiers (SIDs)

Humans prefer to use friendly names when referring to each other, but, of course, these are not unique. How many Pauls or Johns do you know in your workplace or even family? Instead of using usernames when Windows resolves file and folder permissions, Windows uses a unique naming method that provides for each and every object on the computer. We introduced objects earlier, and these can be users, local computers, files, folders, services, printers, etc.

A security identifier (SID) is a unique variable-length numeric value, each beginning with the prefix S, and the various components are separated by hyphens. An example of a SID is as follows:

S-1-5-21-3389011295-2505366984-3037092476-513D

To view an SID on your computer, open an Administrative command prompt and type wmic useraccount get name,sid, as shown in Figure 4-7.

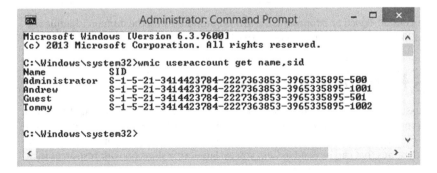

Figure 4-7. Enumerating SIDs for local users

Where SIDs are generated by the same computer, or if the computer is part of a domain, there will be a common base SID component that is consistent throughout the organization. However, the overall SID is unique, and no two user objects will have the same SID.

The digits shown after the last "-" in Figure 4-7 show two default accounts (Administrator and Guest), which are allocated a value less than 1000. All other accounts that are not default have a variable length starting from 1000 and are obtained from the server that issues relative identifier (RID) values. For a non-domain-joined computer, the RID is applied locally. On a local machine and domain controllers, the administrator account will always be -500, and for the guest account, it will be -501. For built-in local users and well-known groups, the SIDs are predefined constants at the beginning of their SID, as shown in Table 4-5.

Table 4-5. *Well-Known SIDs*

SID (starts with)	Well-Known Group	Description
S-1-1-0	Everyone	A group that includes all users except anonymous users
S-1-2-0	Local	Users who log on to terminals locally (physically) connected to the system
S-1-3-0	Creator Owner ID	A temporary security identifier that will be replaced by the SID of the user
S-1-5-500	Administrator	A user account for the system administrator

Because every object has an SID, even your user account, it is often possible to see an SID appear in an ACL or command output, in lieu of the friendly object (i.e., username). This is often seen on slow networks when there is a slight delay resolving the SID to the name.

■ **Link**   A list of well-known SIDs is available at http://support.microsoft.com/ kb/243330.

In a domain-based environment, the SID is combined with the domain identifier to create a 128-bit globally unique identifier (GUID).

NTFS Revisited: Special Identities

We discussed built-in groups within NTFS and how they are useful in enabling the system to set up special groups whose members are allowed to perform tasks such as use Remote Desktop or perform Backup operations. There is another system-generated group of special identities that can be used to help you assign permissions on your resources in an efficient and consistent manner.

Special identities are listed in Table 4-6 and are generally more relevant when assigning permissions to shared resources than directly on local files and folders.

Table 4-6. *Special Identities and Their Descriptions*

Special Identity	Description
Anonymous Logon	Any network logon for which credentials are not provided. Special identity is typically used for web server access when anonymous access to resources is required
Authenticated Users	All users who have successfully logged on to the system with a username and password, but excluding Guest accounts, even if the Guest account uses a password
Creator Owner	A special identity for the account that created a file or folder. Has ultimate authority over the file or folder and normally has Full control permission
Dial Up	User who connects via a dial-up connection
Everyone	All users, including guests, but excluding anonymous users
Interactive	Any user logging on locally, i.e., at the console or through a Remote Desktop Connection
Network	Any user who logs on over the network. Excludes interactive Remote Desktop Connections
Users	Includes authenticated users and domain users. Used in preference to Everyone

It is especially important to review the descriptions for the most common special identities, including Interactive, Authenticated Users, Everyone, and Creator Owner.

■ **Tip**   By default, the Everyone special identity is given access to shared resources. Best practice is to replace Everyone with the Authenticated Users identity.

Physical Security

We have explored many sophisticated methods for protecting your data: "at rest," in Chapter 3, with file permissions, and in this chapter, when data is shared across the network. However, we should also mention the need to ensure that the data is physically safe.

The term *defense-in-depth* is used to describe the use of a layered approach to security. By creating many layers, you reduce the likelihood that an attacker will succeed, as most often, he/she will move on to attack an easier target (with fewer layers of protection). Layers are also proven to increase the detection rate at which you will notice the attack taking place.

Outlined in Table 4-7 are various examples of mitigation actions that an organization can implement for each physical security threat layer.

Table 4-7. *Physical Attack Vectors and Their Mitigations*

Threat Area	Mitigation
Corporate Policies, Procedures, Awareness	Training, bulletins, acceptable use notices, vigilance
Physical Security	Door locks, entry tracking, PIN access, attended reception area, security personnel
Perimeter	Firewalls, Network Access Protection (NAP), Quarantine
Internal Network	VLANs, IPsec, LAN intrusion detection system (IPS), Guest Wi-Fi, MAC Filtering
Host/Client Systems	Firewalls, patching, host-based intrusion detection system, anti-malware, password policy, BitLocker, BitLocker To Go
Application	Application hardening, anti-virus, anti-malware, AppLocker
Data	NTFS, ACLs, Encryption, Digital Rights Management, secure destruction of data storage media

When troubleshooting poor physical or user security, I would suggest taking a short tour around the organization. During the assessment, you should be able to highlight literally dozens of areas that give rise to concern. While it is not expected (or even necessary) that all organizations should implement data center physical security, you should be able to draw up a list of mitigations for each of the areas listed in Table 4-7 and determine those that may have the most significant impact on reducing risk when referring to physical data security.

Some sample measures that can be taken and are often simple (and free) and highly effective in reducing the risk of physical attack include the following:

- Locking the server cabinet or server room and removing the key

- Using Remote Desktop Connection when managing servers

- Preventing the installation of unauthorized applications

- Removing/disabling unnecessary administrative shares

- Using complex passwords and changing them every three to six months

- Discouraging the sharing of user/application passwords and/or implementing multi-factor authentication

- Securing asset tag and alarm hardware in publically accessible areas, such as laptops used in the reception area

- Using BitLocker on all mobile devices (covered in Chapter 5)

- Restricting removable devices, unless protected by BitLocker To Go (covered in Chapter 5)

- Ensuring Windows, anti-virus, and Windows Defender software is patched and up to date

- Ensuring that all users lock their workstations when away from their desks

Most CIOs and IT administrators with whom I have consulted typically do not expect their organizations to be the subject of malicious activity, such as a hacker, data theft, or corporate espionage, and nor should they. The risk of any of these activities in the majority of small- to medium-size businesses is very minimal indeed.

In comparison, the risk of an internal threat of data theft by a disgruntled employee, or data loss through the theft of a laptop, for example, is significantly higher than the threat of corporate espionage.

With this in mind, take another walk around the office and look to see where your potential staff concerns are. Is it the poorly performing salesperson who is awaiting his second and final warning, or the junior help-desk operator who can't remember the administrator password and keeps writing it down in a little book on his desk?

Finally, one last word about physical security. It really does not matter how perfectly you have implemented NTFS or network access security. If you allow a stranger inside your organization to have unmonitored physical access a computer, he/she may not be able to log on to the device and impersonate a member of staff, but before he/she leaves the building (most likely for the last time), he/she can cause a lot of damage nevertheless. Consider the following potential scenarios, in which an employee:

a) Wipes the file server by deleting all partitions, using a boot disk (similar to the boot disk we discuss in Chapter 9)

b) Resets the local Administrator account and gains access to the data stored on a laptop

c) Walks out of the building with the reception computer

Tools

There are several software-based intrusion detection and penetration testing suites available to purchase that will highlight areas of weakness. You could also use hacking software to self-test your network, but we do not recommend this type of testing on your production environment, unless it is carried out by a reputable and recommended IT security professional. Ask your contacts or reach out to your local technology user group and see who is recommended by your peers.

One tool that I will recommend is the Microsoft Baseline Security Analyzer (MBSA), which has been available for a number of years across many versions of Windows. MBSA is a free utility from Microsoft available to download. MBSA 2.3 is the current version, and it is supported on Windows XP through to Windows 8.1 and Windows Server 2012 R2. The tool outputs a user-friendly report that can be used to benchmark devices and lets sysadmins scan local and remote systems for missing patches and common security misconfigurations, as shown in Figure 4-8.

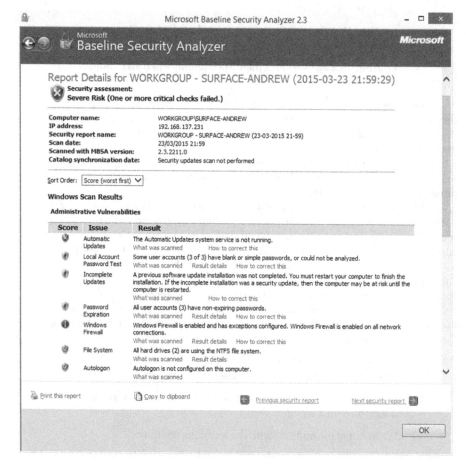

Figure 4-8. Microsoft Baseline Security Analyzer report summary

You can download MBSA at https://www.microsoft.com/en-us/download/details.aspx?id=7558, and more information about MBSA can be found at https://technet.microsoft.com/en-us/security/cc184924.aspx.

In the next chapter, we will cover methods of safeguarding data by using encryption technology to protect your files when they are being stored (data at rest)—either on hard disks or on removable media.

Summary

We have seen throughout this chapter and Chapter 3 that the ability to share files and folders securely across our networks is fundamental to enabling corporations to work effectively and collaboratively.

One of the big challenges faced by all organisations is how should they best secure their data from loss, corruption or theft. This is especially relevant to data that is in transit such as files stored on mobile devices or USB drives. Mainly due to ignorance of what is possible, most businesses do not implement even the basic level of protection for their data. In Chapter 5 we will focus on how to encrypt our data, so that even if it is stolen there will be a high likelihood that it will remain private.

CHAPTER 5

■ ■ ■

Managing and Troubleshooting Encryption

Encryption is the friend we all love to hate. On the one hand, it's an (almost) cast-iron guarantee that when a company server gets hacked or leaks occur, which they do more often than we read about in the news, any data loss won't result in that data being revealed. On the other hand, if something goes wrong with that encryption, all of the valuable data can be lost.

The obvious solution is to keep a separate, unencrypted backup copy of all the data in a secure data vault location somewhere. This can sometimes negate the entire benefit of using encryption in the first instance, however, as many of the major leaks of corporate and governmental data in the last years have resulted from server hacks. Professionally, I have a lot of faith in encryption, and given the choice of leaving confidential data in plain view or encrypting it, encryption would get my vote any day.

As discussed in Chapter 4, you could instead entrust your data to a company much larger, and with a more secure infrastructure, than your own, such as Amazon.com, Microsoft, Google, or Dropbox. To my knowledge, none of these data centers has been hacked, though there's always a weak point of attack, and this is typically the end user. The theft of celebrities' photographs from one such service in 2014 highlighted this problem well, with the owners of those photographs having reportedly used weak passwords.

Passwords are very important when it comes to encryption, and web sites such as that located at www.howsecureismypassword.net provide a way for people to test their strength. These are useful tools to help end users check the strength of their chosen passwords, and resources such as my own video guide to creating secure (and memorable) passwords, pcs.tv/1Da9J9y, encourage people to do just that. However, these are no substitute for a corporate policy that mandates that numbers, symbols, and both upper- and lowercase letters be used in a password that is at least 12 or more characters in length.

Two-factor authentication is a great step forward, with operating systems such as Windows 10 providing multifactor authentication as a baked-in part of the operating system (OS). But two-factor authentication doesn't help with the encryption of files and folders on your own PCs, so it's crucial to ensure that problems don't arise to begin with.

© Mike Halsey and Andrew Bettany 2015
M. Halsey and A. Bettany, *Windows File System Troubleshooting*,
DOI 10.1007/978-1-4842-1016-1_5

Encrypting File System (EFS)

One of the ways to encrypt your files and data in Windows is the first and oldest, the Encrypting File System (EFS). It was first introduced in Windows 2000 and has since been refined. However, it's not without its problems, which I shall come to shortly.

EFS is a file and folder encryption technology; it cannot be used to encrypt an entire hard disk, which means that any disk containing EFS-encrypted files will still be visible to all users of the PC, even if they can't open and read the content.

You can encrypt any file or folder on an NTFS-formatted hard disk by right-clicking it and selecting Properties from the context menu that appears. Next, click the Advanced button on the first General tab, and encryption options will appear (see Figure 5-1).

Figure 5-1. *You can encrypt and decrypt files from their Properties inspector*

You can also decrypt files from the same dialog, and both processes are performed by simply checking or unchecking a single box and clicking OK.

Encrypting any files or folders with EFS will automatically create an Encryption Key, and a pop-up alert in your system tray will prompt you to make a copy of this. This key is necessary to unlock the files should a new user be logged on to the machine—the current copy of Windows being restored from a backup—or if the files are moved or copied to another PC.

Within a corporate environment, administrators normally restrict the ability for users to arbitrarily encrypt files, unless there is a strong business case for encryption to be used. EFS is a powerful tool, and often, users are unaware of the potential issues that can occur if EFS is poorly managed. EFS can be restricted by using Group Policy (review the settings in the Computer Configuration ➤ Windows Settings ➤ Security Settings ➤ Public Key Policies ➤ Encrypting File System GPO). Where EFS is allowed, it is essential that an Encrypted Data Recovery Agent (DRA) be created prior to EFS first being used. A DRA is a special user right (normally allocated to the administrator) that is able to decrypt data that has been encrypted by other users.

▪ **Note**   Normally, once a file has been encrypted using EFS, only the owner/user who encrypted it, or a DRA, will have access to the file. If a user encrypts a file using EFS before the DRA has been created, the file will not be able to be decrypted by the DRA.

Should you be encrypting a file within a folder that is unencrypted, Windows 8 and newer versions will alert you that software in which you open the file, or other actions performed on that folder, might create unencrypted copies of the file that can then be accessed (see Figure 5-2).

Figure 5-2. *You will be warned if your encryption can be compromised*

When you click the option to back up your file encryption key, you will additionally be asked if this is something you want to do right then (which I cannot recommend highly enough), if you want to back it up later, or if you don't care about the data and don't mind losing access to it completely (see Figure 5-3). Not backing up the key straight away, or not having Windows reminding you the next time you start your PC, can in some cases lead to the key being forgotten about and not backed up at all. Should the PC then be reimaged, or the OS reinstalled, that key will be lost forever, and access to your encrypted files will become impossible, unless you pay for expensive decryption services.

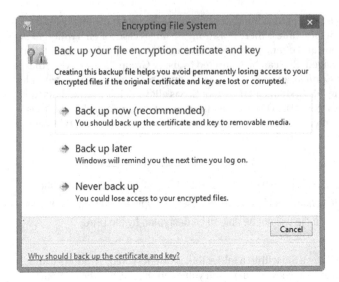

Figure 5-3. *EFS asks when you want to back up your encryption key*

Backing up your encryption key displays the Certificate Export Wizard, which will walk you through several steps, the first of which is choosing the file format you want your certificate to take (see Figure 5-4).

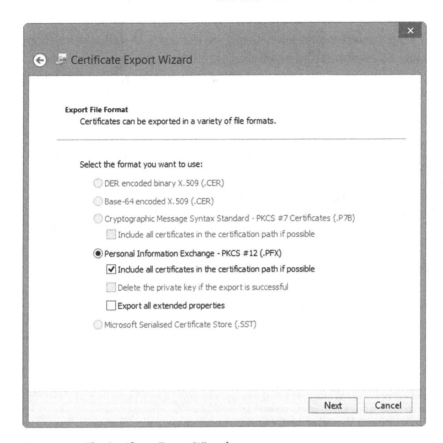

Figure 5-4. *The Certificate Export Wizard*

In the example here, the .PFX, Personal Information Exchange file that will be exported contains the private (personal) key; the other options become available when you are also exporting the public key.

There are two options with this certificate type: Include all certificates in the certification path if possible and Export all extended properties (which is only really used if you want to decrypt the files and folders using a non-Windows OS, such as when troubleshooting Windows from a bootable Linux disc). Naturally, the latter of these two options, to include all relevant information within the certificate, will provide a better guarantee of unlocking the files later, regardless of whether you choose any additional properties or parameters for the encryption. I say this because of the "better safe than sorry" rule, and for no other reason.

Next, you will be prompted for a password, and this is potentially the weakest point and a possible attack vector for encryption. The password you use when securing the encryption keys should always contain a mixture of upper- and lowercase characters, numbers, and symbols. To achieve a strong password, the length should be a minimum of 12 characters. Some ideas for how to help make passwords more secure, while keeping them memorable, follow.

■ **Note**   Some numbers and symbols can easily, and memorably, be substituted for letters in a password. For example, () can be used instead of o, O, or 0 (zero), $ can be substituted for s, # for h, / for 7, & for a, ^ for v, and so on. You can also use rules, such as capitalizing the second, third, or last letter of each word, instead of the first, and build your passwords around phrases to make them stronger still.

Last, you will be asked for a location and a file name for the exported key. You might want to name this key after the user of the PC on which the encrypted files are located. **DO NOT** ever, however, store this key in a location that is encrypted by EFS, as you may lose access to it and be unable to decrypt your files later.

You manage your file encryption certificates and keys at any time by searching for **encrypt** in the Start menu, or at the Start screen, and selecting Manage File Encryption Certificates from the options that appear.

On selecting this option, the Encrypting File System wizard (see Figure 5-5) will appear.

Figure 5-5. The Encrypting File System wizard

Here, you can back up existing, or even create new, EFS encryption certificates. You will be asked which certificate you wish to work with and then be given options to view the certificate details and back up the certificate and encryption key.

You can reimport an EFS encryption certificate and key at any time and on any compatible PC, by opening the certificate file and typing the appropriate password.

If you are using a Microsoft account (Windows 8 and newer versions), your EFS certificates are roamed between your devices—a feature called Credential Roaming. Any usernames, passwords, certificates, and smart card information that you allow Windows to remember is stored within the Credential Manager, which is a secure area of the user account profile. On trusted devices, these credentials are automatically synchronized when you sign in to the device using your Microsoft account. To view your Credential Manager and its contents, open Control Panel, User Accounts and Family Safety, and then select Credential Manager. Alternatively, search for Credential from the Start screen.

▪ **Note**   You can manually enforce or disable the synchronization of passwords, using Group Policy. In the Group Policy Editor, you will find the settings at Computer Configuration ➤ Administrative Templates ➤ Windows Components ➤ Sync Your Settings.

Managing EFS Keys in the Microsoft Management Console (MMC)

You can additionally manage EFS encryption keys in the Microsoft Management Console, by searching for *mmc* at the Start menu or Start screen.

In order to import, export, or manage keys, you have to add the Certificates snap-in to the console, and you do this in the File menu by selecting Add/Remove Snap-in. Next, you should select Certificates from the list of available snap-ins, click the Add button, and then ensure that the Current User Certificate store is selected (see Figure 5-6).

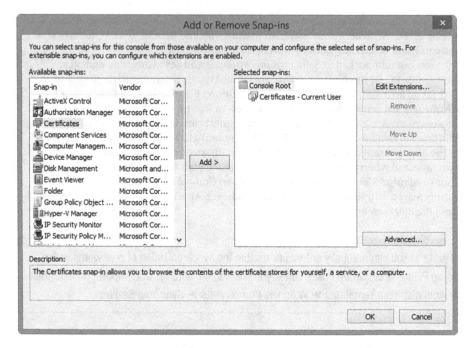

Figure 5-6. *You have to add the Certificate snap-in to the MMC*

Once you have successfully added the certificates snap-in, you will find your EFS certificates listed under Certificates ➤ Current User ➤ Personal ➤ Certificates (see Figure 5-7).

Figure 5-7. *Managing EFS certificates in the MMC*

Opening a certificate in the MMC and clicking its Details tab allows you to make a backup copy of the certificate, using the Copy to File button (see Figure 5-8).

Figure 5-8. *You can back up the EFS key in its Certificate Inspector*

EFS and CIPHER.EXE

In addition to the MMC and the Encryption Certificate Wizard, Windows comes with a command-line utility called `cipher.exe`. This utility can be used to encrypt and decrypt files and folders, as well as manage encryption keys.

You must open a command prompt window with elevated, Administrator privileges and use it in the following format and with the following switches:

```
CIPHER [{/e | /d}] [/s:Folder] [options] [/u[/n]] [{Pathname [...]]]
```

> **/e**—Encrypt the specified folders and their enclosed files.

> **/d**—Decrypt the specified folders and their enclosed files.

/s:Folder—Perform the action on the folder and all sub-folders and files within the subfolders.

/a—Perform the operation for both files and folders.

/i—Do not stop in the event of an error occurring.

/f—Force the encryption or decryption of all files and folders (the default action is to skip items that have already been encrypted).

/q—Quiet mode, report only essential information.

/h—Display files that have their hidden or system attribute checked; normally, these files are not encrypted.

/k—Create a new file encryption key for the current user.

/u—Update an existing file encryption key with the new data (this option only works with /n).

/n—Prevent file encryption keys from being updated (this option only works with /u and can be used to find all encrypted files on the local drives).

/C—Display additional information on the type of encryption used.

Additionally, the following command-line switches can be used:

/r:PathnameWithoutFileExtension—Create a new encryption certificate and key and write this key to the path specified.

/w:Pathname—Permanently remove deleted files from the specified path, this includes files not previously encrypted using EFS.

/x[:Pathname] PathnameWithoutExtension—Make a backup copy of the certificates and private keys for the current user to a .pfx file.

/adduser [username]—Add the specified user to the access rights for an encrypted file.

/removeuser [username]—Remove the user's right to access an encrypted file.

/rekey—Update encrypted files to use your current EFS key.

In addition, cipher.exe can be used on its own, in a command prompt, to report a list of all the encrypted files and folders in that path (see Figure 5-9).

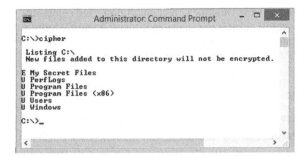

Figure 5-9. *Using* `cipher.exe` *to list the encryption status of files and folders*

The Limitations of EFS

I mentioned at the beginning of this section on EFS that this encryption system is not without its concerns. Chief among these is the primary advantage of EFS: that files remain encrypted even after they are copied or moved away from the encrypted folder.

"But this is a benefit" I hear you cry! It is—so long as you realize that EFS is only supported on volumes formatted with the NTFS file system. If you are not using NTFS, the warning is stark: Be careful! This means that copying or moving an encrypted file to a disk formatted with a different file system, such as UDF on a DVD, exFAT on a USB flash drive, or HFS+ on a Mac, can result in the files being unencrypted and, in some rare cases, the entire file becoming scrambled and undecryptable. I have encountered this myself on a Linux-based network attached storage (NAS) drive that used its own proprietary file system, and, boy, was it annoying!

As the owner of encrypted files, you are able to open, decrypt, move, copy, and delete the files. Another user may be able to see the existence of the files, but unless they have access to your encryption key, they are unable to open or unencrypt any encrypted file that you have created.

Additionally, EFS is hamstrung by being only a file- and folder-encryption system. If you allow access to the underlying file system on the disk, the details of the files, including their file names and their properties, could be accessed by unauthorized users, which could give attackers valuable insight into the nature of the files and allow them to target their resources on files that appear to be most valuable. For mobile devices and removable data drives, which by their nature are not easily protected once they leave the enterprise, it is worth considering using Microsoft's BitLocker drive encryption system.

BitLocker and BitLocker To Go

Microsoft's BitLocker drive encryption system works differently from EFS, being a full-volume encryption technology instead of a file and folder encryption technology. It takes advantage of the emergence of newer technologies, such as Trusted Platform Module (TPM) chips, which have become commonplace on tablets and laptops of all shapes and sizes. BitLocker To Go is a special version of BitLocker that can encrypt removable media such as USB flash drives. Both of these tools have a reputation for bringing peace of mind to mobile workers who need to store valuable or regulation-protected company or customer data while on the move. BitLocker is not available in all versions of Windows. It has been marketed as a business feature, and, therefore, it is available in the Enterprise and Ultimate editions of Windows Vista and Windows 7 and the Pro and Enterprise editions of Windows 8 and 8.1

■ **Note** BitLocker To Go does not require a TPM to work, but drives encrypted using it will be read-only on some operating systems, such as Windows XP and Windows Vista, which do not support the creation or writing of data to BitLocker To Go devices. For example, Vista will require you to use the BitLocker To Go Reader (`bitlockertogo.exe`), which is present on the flash drive and is used when the drive is plugged into the PC. You can find out more about the BitLocker To Go Reader software for Vista and Windows XP at `http://pcs.tv/1Dnx1uC`.

BitLocker is so secure that rumor has it that during its development, the US State Department and Pentagon reportedly asked Microsoft to place a back door into the system, a request that was refused by Microsoft.

BitLocker is managed from the Control Panel, and the main BitLocker console displays commands for managing BitLocker, as well as the status of your current drives, be they encrypted or unencrypted (see Figure 5-10).

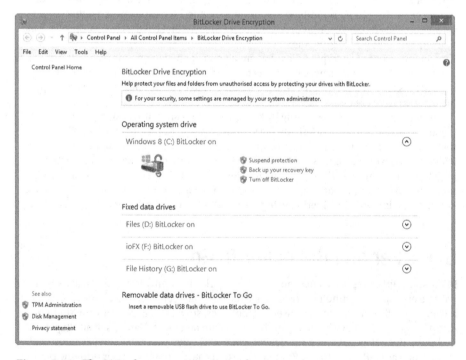

Figure 5-10. *The BitLocker management console*

You can encrypt both hard disks (internal and external, such as USB) and portable drives (such as USB flash drives) with BitLocker, the latter being known as *BitLocker To Go*. When you encrypt a drive using BitLocker, you are asked several questions.

If you do not have a TPM chip in which your encryption key(s) will be stored, Windows will ask you either to add a password to secure your recovery key or to specify a smart card that will be used to unlock the drive (see Figure 5-11).

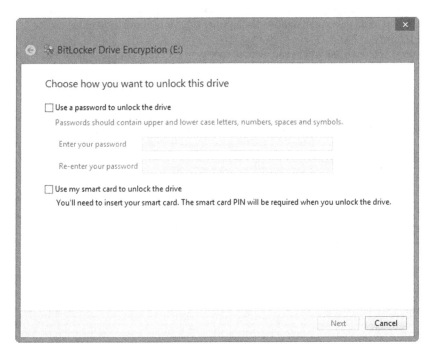

Figure 5-11. *Adding unlock mechanisms to BitLocker*

BitLocker comes with its own password policy, meaning that short and insecure passwords simply cannot be used. This helps to provide an additional layer of security and peace of mind to system administrators.

■ **Note** To encrypt your Windows drive, you can use BitLocker on PCs that do not have a TPM chip, by changing a setting in Group Policy in the Windows Pro and Enterprise editions. Run gpedit.msc from the Start menu or Start screen search box, and in the Group Policy editor, navigate to Computer Configuration ➤ Administrative Templates ➤ Windows Components ➤ Bit Locker Drive Encryption ➤ Operating System Drives. Here, open the Require Additional Authentication at Startup policy, enable it, and then you will be able to check the option Allow BitLocker without a compatible TPM.

Other options can appear in this dialog, depending on the type of drive you are encrypting and the hardware you have installed. If you are encrypting a physical hard disk that is installed in the PC, the option to unlock the drive using a USB flash drive (which will have to be plugged into the PC whenever the hard disk is accessed) will appear.

For internal hard disks and partitions in a PC that you encrypt, if you have a TPM chip in your PC, and if the drive or partition containing your Windows installation is also encrypted with BitLocker, you will be asked if you want to "Automatically unlock this drive on this computer," with the "on this computer" part being significant, as the hard disk will remain encrypted if moved to another PC. More about TPM chips will be discussed shortly.

Windows will then ask where you want to save your recovery key (see Figure 5-12).

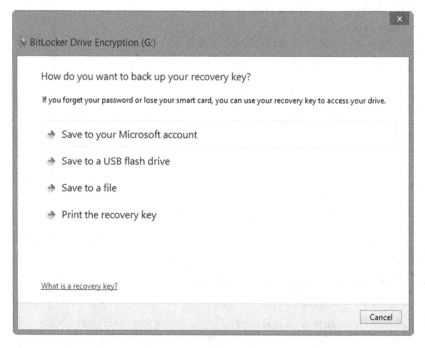

Figure 5-12. Saving your BitLocker recovery key

■ **Note**   If you use a Microsoft account to store your recovery key, it can be found online at https://onedrive.live.com/recoverykey.

The options listed are for a hard disk that is being encrypted and will change depending on your login type and the type of drive you are encrypting. For example, encrypting a USB flash drive will not offer the option of saving the encryption key to another USB flash drive, and logging into a Windows 8 PC using a local account or a domain without Connected Account functionality will not display the option to save the key to your Microsoft account (this option is not available in Vista or Windows 7).

The next option is probably the most interesting, as you are asked if you want to encrypt the entire drive or just the current used disk space (see Figure 5-13). Both options will encrypt the data on the drive, and the used disk space option is useful during deployment, as this can significantly speed up the provisioning of BitLocker on newly commissioned devices. This option was introduced in Windows 8 and newer versions and, therefore, does not appear if you are using Windows 7.

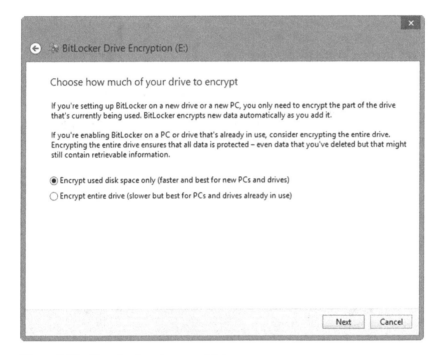

Figure 5-13. *Choosing how to encrypt drives*

BitLocker and TPM Chips

The TPM is a motherboard chip that comes preinstalled or can be added via a plug-in module, and it is used to store encryption keys. The TPM (1.2 and newer versions) is used by BitLocker to store information that ties the hard drive to the motherboard and securely holds the volume master key, which BitLocker requires once the computer has verified the status of the TPM chip and that the drive has been removed from the computer.

To use a TPM chip with your PC, you first have to activate it, which you can do in the BitLocker management panel, by clicking the TPM Administration link at the bottom-left corner of the window (see Figure 5-14).

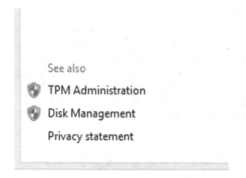

Figure 5-14. *Accessing TPM Administration*

This will display a management console in which the TPM chip can be activated and managed. The commands for performing these actions will appear in the right panel of the window (see Figure 5-15) and includes preparing the TPM for use, turning it off, changing the default password for the chip, and clearing it.

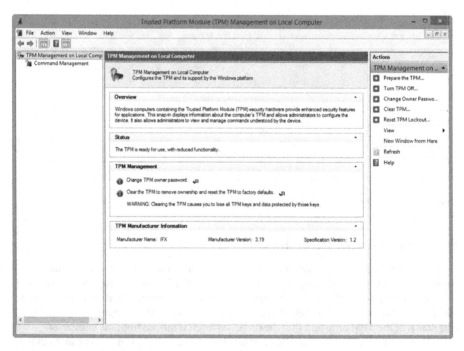

Figure 5-15. *Administering a TPM chip*

Change TPM Owner Password allows you to change the password for the TPM chip itself. This is set by Windows when the chip is activated and is required for all administrative actions thereafter. Additionally, the Reset TPM Lockout option will deactivate the security that the chip implements, if it feels it has been tampered with.

Throughout the history of Windows, it has always been possible to remove a hard drive from a faulty, stolen, or lost device and simply attach it to another computer, and the user is able to read the data contained on the disk. The only protection against this is to use encryption. With BitLocker, should a hard disk on which data has been encrypted with BitLocker, and on which the encryption keys are stored in a TPM chip, be removed from the PC, the disk will be unreadable (i.e., it remains fully encrypted) until reinserted in the original PC or unlocked using the BitLocker recovery key for the disk.

BitLocker and Windows RT

For those managing devices that run the ARM processor version of Windows, you won't find BitLocker in the Control Panel. Instead, in PC Settings, under PC and Devices and then PC Info, you will see Device encryption (see Figure 5-16).

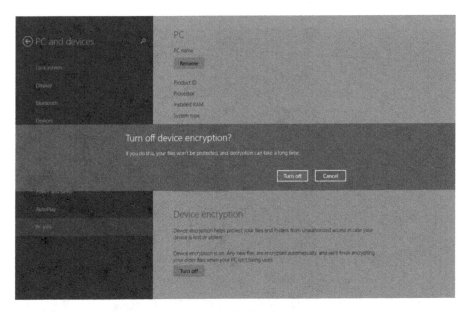

Figure 5-16. In Windows RT, BitLocker is called Device encryption

This is a full disk encryption system based on BitLocker and comes activated by default on all Windows RT systems, if you use a Microsoft account with the device. It can be deactivated should you wish, though it adds valuable extra security to the device. Because this is a consumer device, there are no management tools available to the user, apart from turn on or off.

If you do not use a Microsoft account with the device, this feature will be disabled, as it does not offer any way other than through your Microsoft account to keep a backup copy of the recovery key.

The Limitations of BitLocker

As is the case of EFS, BitLocker is not without its problems and limitations. Sometimes, BitLocker can throw a bit of a curve and require you to enter your unlock key at boot time (see Figure 5-17). It can be handy, therefore, if you are traveling, either to keep a web page link on your smartphone to the BitLocker recovery key that is stored in your Microsoft account at https://onedrive.live.com/recoverykey or to keep a USB flash drive with a copy of the recovery key handy (but not in the same place as your laptop or tablet!).

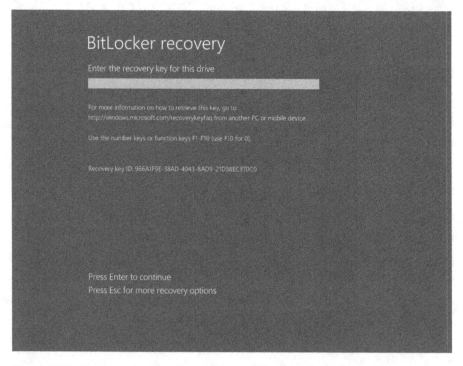

Figure 5-17. *Windows can ask you to enter your BitLocker recovery key at boot time*

Additionally, it's important to stress that BitLocker is completely incompatible with dual-boot systems and will require you to reenter your Recovery key every time you start the OS, if this is how your system is configured. This can be a pain, as the Recovery key is 48 characters long.

Again, as with EFS, BitLocker only supports disks formatted with the NTFS. BitLocker To Go will, however, encrypt your removable drives, which can be formatted in a variety of file formats, including NTFS, FAT32, FAT, and exFAT formatted USB flash drives. Last, with BitLocker, is that because it's the drive that is encrypted and not the files, any file copied or moved away from that disk is automatically decrypted. While not a limitation in itself, it might not be clear to a nontechnical user that the copy of the file(s) he/she has created are no longer encrypted.

Recovering Encrypted Data

As you might expect me to say at this point, recovering files and data that have been encrypted using either EFS or BitLocker (or indeed any other encryption technology, such as TrueCrypt) isn't easy, and it isn't designed to be. Troubleshooting encryption is all about prevention.

Within a corporate environment, deploying BitLocker must be carefully planned and managed. Microsoft provides support for Microsoft BitLocker Administration and Monitoring (MBAM) as part of the Microsoft Desktop Optimization Pack (MDOP), a suite of utilities for Software Assurance customers. The latest version of the tool, at the time of writing, MBAM 2.5, offers administrators a graphical user interface (GUI) to manage BitLocker, including reporting on the encryption status of individual computers or across the whole enterprise, and the ability to access recovery key information when users are locked out of their devices.

Some companies offer services that will decrypt EFS and BitLocker-encrypted files and disks, but they are expensive, and all require a brute-force attack on the encryption, which can be slowed further (pushing the price up), if you have sensibly used a very secure password that you can't remember.

In short, it is far better to maintain a safe copy of your backup key in a repository, such as a Microsoft account or a secure store in a Windows Server system, than it is to find yourself locked out of crucial files and data.

Summary

Encryption is a double-edged sword that's eased significantly by the very need to have our data safe and secure from thieves. Data protection laws around the world are extremely strict and designed to safeguard the personal and private information of the people who entrust you with it. The fines for losing unencrypted data can be severe and enough to put smaller companies out of business altogether.

Encryption in Windows *is* easy to deploy and manage, however, and with careful planning and a safe repository for the keys, it is an extremely effective way to secure your data and your company's future.

CHAPTER 6

■ ■ ■

Troubleshooting the Windows File System

So far in this book, we've detailed the complexities of the Windows file system and some of the most common problems you can encounter with files, such as security and access permissions.

These actions would be performed on your user files and documents, however, so what would you do if Windows system files, or those for programs or drivers, were to become corrupt?

Fortunately, Windows provides a few ways to deal with this problem, either automatically or by helping you to repair files manually.

The System File Checker

Windows contains a few hidden gems, such as the Problem Steps Recorder (search for PSR), at the Start menu or Start screen, which can record annotated screen grabs of problems that can be sent to a support technician, and the Clean Boot Mode, which is a halfway house between the very limited functionality of Safe Mode and the full desktop experience. You can find the Diagnostic startup mode in the System Configuration (MSConfig.exe) panel.

One of the most useful tools in relation to troubleshooting Windows, however, is the System File Checker (SFC.exe; see Figure 6-1).

© Mike Halsey and Andrew Bettany 2015

M. Halsey and A. Bettany, *Windows File System Troubleshooting*,
DOI 10.1007/978-1-4842-1016-1_6

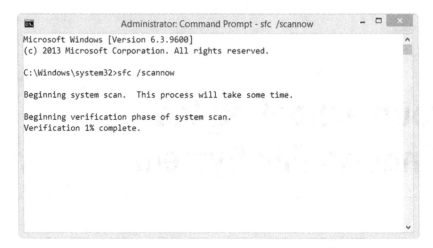

Figure 6-1. *The System File Checker tool*

The System File Checker scans all the files that make up your installed Windows operating system (OS) for integrity and reports on any that have been changed, are missing, or are corrupt. Windows will replace any files that are damaged or missing with a cached copy that is stored in a compressed folder at C:\Windows\winsxs\Backup.

To use it, you will need a Windows installation DVD (it doesn't work with USB flash drives), and that DVD must have the current version of Windows that you are using, including the integrated copy of the currently installed service pack on your PC.

■ **Note**   If you subscribe to Microsoft's MSDN of Software Assurance services, you can download Windows ISO files with integrated service packs. Should these not be available, you can get third-party software, such as the excellent RT7Lite in Windows 7 or WinReducer in Windows 8.1, which will integrate service packs into an existing Windows ISO file.

To use the System File Checker, type the command SFC /SCANNOW into a command prompt (Admin) window. If you have your Windows installation DVD in your PC and the System File Checker finds a problem, it will automatically copy the original file from the disk, replacing the faulty file on the PC.

There are also additional command-line switches that you can use with the System File Checker.

> **/VERIFYONLY** will report on any corrupt or missing files but won't attempt to repair them.

> **/SCANFILE** can be used to check and repair the integrity of an individual file and can be used in the format sfc /scanfile=c:\Windows\System32\file.dll.

/VERIFYFILE is used in the same format as the `/scanfile` switch but only verifies the integrity of the file.

/OFFBOOTDIR is used to verify the boot files for the PC. This can be useful if the boot system (perhaps a dual-boot PC) is misbehaving or is corrupt. If you are starting your PC from media such as a System repair disk, recovery drive, Windows To Go stick, or the Windows installation DVD, use the syntax `sfc /offbootdir=d:\`, where D: is the location of your Windows installation. We will cover repairing the Windows boot files in depth in Chapter 7.

/OFFWINDIR is used similarly to `/offbootdir` but scans the /Windows folder on your hard disk for errors. To use offline from bootable media, use the format `sfc /offwindir=d:\ Windows`.

If the System File Checker finds corrupt files but cannot repair them, it will report this in its log file, which you can find at `%windir%\Logs\CBS\CBS.log` (see Figure 6-2).

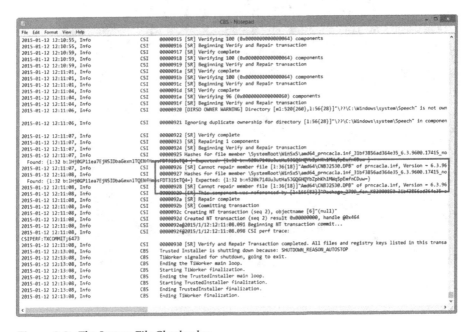

Figure 6-2. *The System File Checker log*

You will see in the example shown in Figure 6-2 that SFC is reporting that the files AMD64\CNBJ2630.DPB and AMD64\32530.DPB in prncacla.inf *cannot be repaired.*

This might have been because I didn't have my Windows install DVD in the drive when I ran the System File Checker, or it could have been because the DVD didn't include the most recently installed service pack. Perhaps it could have been because these are driver files downloaded from Windows Update or the AMD web site after Windows had been installed and that were not included in the OS installation media.

Reading the Blue Screen of Death

If your PC is suffering from the dreaded Blue Screen of Death, you can still get useful information should a file be the cause. In Figures 6-3 and 6-4, you can see that the files SPCMDCON.SYS and pci.sys, respectively, have been reported by Windows as having caused the blue screen.

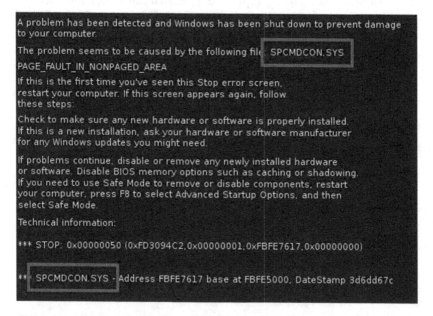

Figure 6-3. The Blue Screen of Death provides useful information

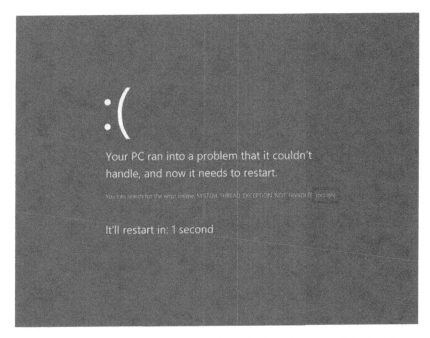

Figure 6-4. *The Windows 8 Blue Screen of Death also informs you if the fault is an offending file*

A search in the PC or a quick search online can reveal the purpose and location of the file, and you might find that it's one that can be updated, perhaps by reinstalling a program or either updating or rolling back a system driver, or fixed with the System File Checker.

If you can't start Windows at all after a Blue Screen of Death, all is not lost, and in Chapter 9, we'll detail how to repair a non-bootable copy of Windows on a file-by-file basis.

Discovering Driver Files

Hardware driver files can often be the biggest problem when it comes to causing Windows to become unstable and crash, especially ones that are loaded very early in the boot process, such as your graphics driver.

The Device Manager in Windows is extremely good at reporting all the files associated with a specific driver, however. To access this information, open the driver properties panel in Device Manager, and under the Driver tab click the Driver Details button.

This will reveal a complete list of all the files that make up that specific driver, together with their file location and name (see Figure 6-5).

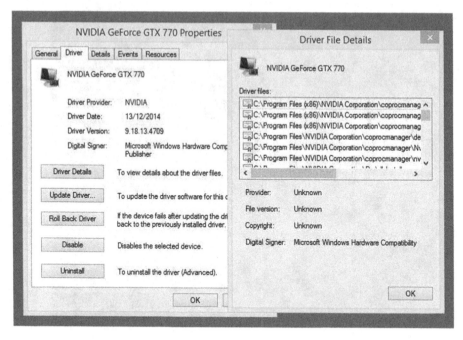

Figure 6-5. *The Device Manager can report all the files associated with a device driver*

This can be useful if you have to remove all the files for a driver manually, perhaps because updating or rolling back the driver isn't fixing the problem, or reinstalling or updating the driver is reporting a problem with the driver that is already installed.

Safe Mode and Diagnostic Startup

If you can't repair Windows file problems from the desktop in normal mode, there are other options available to you. You will likely be familiar with Safe Mode, which has been available in Windows for many versions now and loads Windows in a reduced-functionality mode, without any third-party drivers or startup software.

You can access Safe Mode from the boot options menu by pressing the F8 key at startup, after the BIOS/EFI information has disappeared but before the Windows logo appears.

With Windows 8, however, the time available to press this button is just milliseconds, but if you're able to boot into Windows, hold down the Shift key and hit Restart to automatically restart the PC and force Windows into the boot and recovery menu options when the PC restarts.

With Windows Vista and Windows 7, the Safe Mode option is listed in the main boot options menu, but it can be harder to find in Windows 8.

1. At the main Windows 8 recovery screen, first click Troubleshoot.

2. At the next screen, click Advanced options.

3. Finally, click Startup Settings.

You will now be shown what settings will be available to you and prompted to restart the PC.

The menu that will then appear (see Figure 6-6) contains the options that you will see automatically by pressing F8 in Windows Vista and Windows 7. These include Enable Safe Mode and Disable automatic restart after failure (to prevent an automatic restart on a Blue Screen of Death).

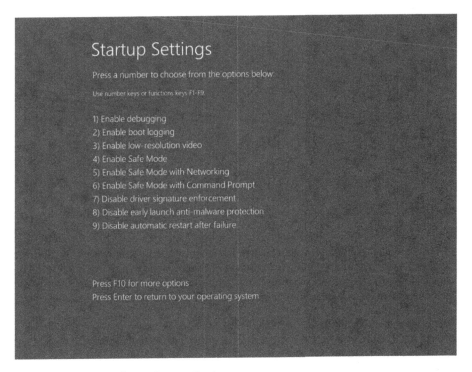

Figure 6-6. The Windows 8 Startup Settings menu

Diagnostic Mode

I mentioned Diagnostic mode earlier in this chapter, and you can activate it from the System Configuration panel (see Figure 6-7) by typing "MSConfig" at the Start menu or Start screen.

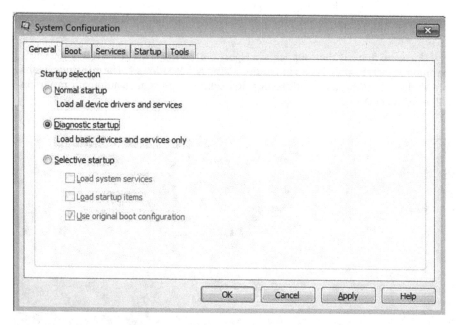

Figure 6-7. *The MSConfig panel*

Safe Mode in Windows is useful but extremely limited. For example, some Control Panel and Administrative options (such as the Windows Defender antivirus application in Windows 8.1, the network and sharing center, and user-specific controls) are simply not available, due to the reduced number of device drivers and services that are loaded when using Safe Mode.

Diagnostic mode, however (see Figure 6-8), is a halfway house between Safe Mode and the full desktop experience, and it has many advantages over Safe Mode, if your PC is able to boot into Windows

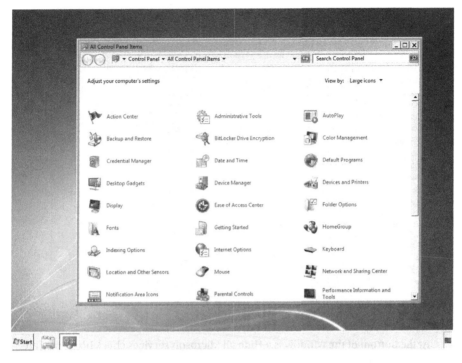

Figure 6-8. *Windows Diagnostic mode*

For example, not only are all your Control Panel options available, but you are able to use the full resolution of your screen, without being limited to the very low resolution that is used when using Safe Mode.

Choosing Diagnostic mode will force Windows to start this way every time it boots. To boot normally to the desktop, you will need to go back into the System Configuration panel and check Normal startup.

Additionally in Diagnostic startup, you can disable Startup programs and both Windows services and third-party services, should they be causing problems on the PC or if you won't need them during your diagnostic phase.

To disable startup programs in Windows Vista and Windows 7, click the Startup tab in System Configuration and uncheck the items you want to disable. In Windows 8, open the Task Manager and click the Startup tab. Then, select the app you want to disable and click the Disable button in the bottom right of the window.

To disable Windows and third-party services from running at startup, in the System Configuration panel click the Services tab (see Figure 6-9). Here you will see a list of all services within the OS, with their current status. Note that Services that are listed as Stopped likely do not start at boot time.

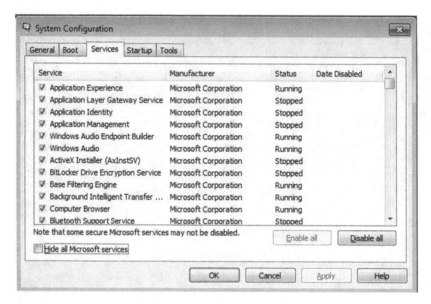

Figure 6-9. *Disabling Windows Services at startup*

At the bottom of the window is a Hide all Microsoft services check box. This can be useful in helping you identify only third-party services. You can check the services you want to disable and then click the Disable all button, to disable the checked services.

Remember that just as with the Diagnostic startup, once you have troubleshooted the problem, you may need to re-enable any disabled services that are still required afterward, when you want to start the PC normally.

Forcing Safe Mode

If you want to force Windows to boot into Safe Mode, you can choose this option within the System Configuration tool under the Boot tab by checking the Safe boot option (see Figure 6-10).

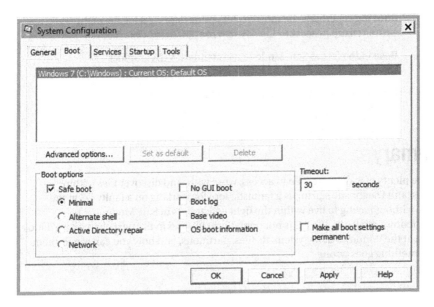

Figure 6-10. *Forcing Safe Mode in Windows*

Just as with Diagnostic startup, checking this option will force the PC to start into Safe Mode every time the PC boots. You will have to uncheck the Safe boot option to return to normal startup.

You will see that other options are available for use with Safe Mode in Windows.

- **Safe boot: Minimal** opens Safe Mode, running critical Windows services only.

- **Safe boot: Alternate shell** opens the Command Prompt with Windows running critical service only. In this mode, both networking and the file explorer are disabled.

- **Safe boot: Active Directory repair** is used for troubleshooting a Domain Controller within a corporate environment. Selecting this option loads the Active Directory services, to allow for offline repair of the AD services and files.

- **Safe boot: Network** runs Safe Mode with critical services and with networking enabled.

- **No GUI boot** does not display the Windows welcome screen when starting.

- **Boot log** is perhaps the most useful option, storing a log file of the entire startup process in the %systemroot%Ntbtlog.txt file.

- **Base video** forces Safe Mode to use standard VGA graphics drivers.

- **OS boot information** displays driver names as they are loaded at startup.

Summary

There are plenty of ways to be able to access, work with, and discover files within Windows, and Diagnostic startup is a fantastic tool for working on a faulty OS at the desktop, without having to live within the tight constraints of Safe Mode.

Sometimes, however, the PC is not bootable at all, and in the next chapter, we'll look in-depth at the Windows boot system, its files, partitions, and how you can repair them when something goes wrong.

CHAPTER 7

■ ■ ■

Troubleshooting the Windows Boot Files

Having a PC that won't boot is one of the most frustrating and worrisome problems anyone can encounter. With other PC and Windows issues, it's usually clear what the problem is: a software package not working or a misconfigured network connection. When the PC won't boot, however, you're left completely in the dark as to the cause, which can be anything from corrupt boot files to a hardware failure.

Fortunately, PC hardware is extremely resilient and long-lasting these days. Often, nowadays, these won't be causes of non-booting systems. The Windows boot system is more likely the cause. But this boot system is hidden away, kept under high levels of security to prevent infection by malware and rootkits and not often detailed in technical books...at least not until now.

The Windows Boot Partitions

The boot files in Windows are kept in hidden and secure partitions located before your Windows installation, the configuration of which will vary depending on whether your motherboard has a BIOS or EFI management system.

■ **Note** It should be noted that versions of Windows up to and including XP do not include separate boot partitions, instead relying on a far more insecure boot.ini file at the root of the Windows partition.

For PC systems with a traditional Basic Input/Output System (BIOS) on the motherboard, the Windows installer creates a *System Reserved* partition of 100MB in size before the Windows partition (see Figure 7-1), in which it stores all the boot. This partition and its contents are hidden from user view, though you can both view and edit the System Reserved partition if you boot from an OS-on-a-disk, such as GNU/Linux.

© Mike Halsey and Andrew Bettany 2015
M. Halsey and A. Bettany, *Windows File System Troubleshooting*,
DOI 10.1007/978-1-4842-1016-1_7

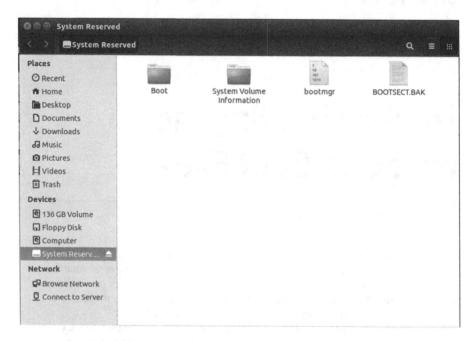

Figure 7-1. The BIOS System Reserved partition

For systems with an Extensible Firmware Interface (EFI) motherboard, the Windows installer creates three system partitions: a 100MB *EFI System* partition (see Figure 7-2), a 300MB *Recovery* partition that contains a copy of the WINRE (Windows Recovery Environment) file, and a third small, hidden partition that's used for storing security tools, such as those used for BitLocker drive encryption.

■ **Note** If your PC has a 32-bit only CPU, you may only see a System Reserved partition, even with an EFI firmware system on the motherboard. This is because of a lack of EFI support from some PC makers for 32-bit chipsets.

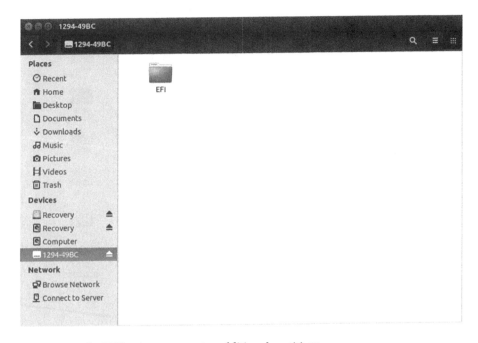

Figure 7-2. *The EFI boot system creates additional partitions*

When repairing the Windows boot files, you'll only want to work with the EFI System partition, and even booting your PC from a GNU/Linux CD, as I have done for these screenshots, will deny you access to the Security partition.

Regardless of the BIOS/EFI system you have on your PC, the contents of the System Reserved and EFI System partitions (see Figure 7-3) are broadly the same (see Figure 7-4).

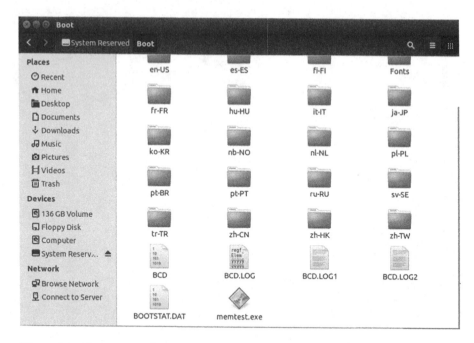

Figure 7-3. *The contents of the System Reserved partition*

Both partitions contain language folders for the recovery tools. Additionally, they both contain the main boot information file (BCD), some log files, and a memory test application that can be used within the recovery environment to test the PC's physical memory for faults.

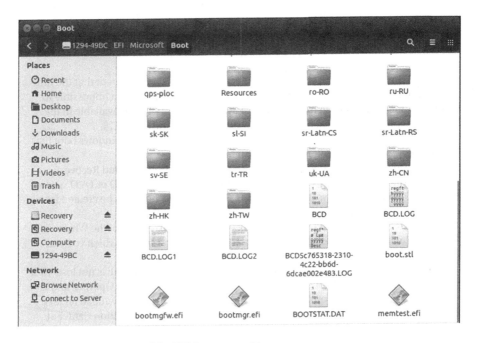

Figure 7-4. *The contents of the EFI System partition*

Additionally, the EFI System partition contains some files specifically used by EFI systems that manage features not supported by BIOS.

If you are viewing the System partitions from a portable operating system (OS) such as GNU/Linux, you can make backup copies of the files, or, indeed, the entire partitions, using a disk imaging tool. These can later be restored or perhaps copied from another identical PC in your workplace that is configured similarly.

Accessing the Windows Recovery Environment

There are several ways to access the Windows Recovery Environment, and the methods used will vary, depending on the version of Windows you are using.

■ **Note**   The Recovery Environment for Windows XP is quite different from that seen in Windows Vista and later versions, and we won't be covering it here, owing to Windows XP and all earlier versions of the OS being out of support and unsupported by security and other patches and updates.

It's normal to press the F8 key on your keyboard after the BIOS/EFI messages have disappeared from your screen, and before the Windows logo appears, to launch the Boot Options Menu. From here, you can select Repair your computer to access the Recovery tools.

With Windows 8, Microsoft sped up the boot system to such an extent that the time available to press F8 was reduced to just milliseconds, making it almost impossible to hit in time, meaning you will have to create a System Recovery Drive (available in the Recovery applet in the Control Panel), from which you can start the PC.

You may find yourself in a circumstance, however, in which the Windows boot files are so corrupt that the boot options menu isn't available.

This is where tools such as the System Rescue Disc (Windows 7) and Recovery Drive (Windows 8) are useful. The System Rescue Disc is a bootable CD or DVD, and a Recovery Drive, for Windows 8, is a bootable USB flash drive. Both can be created from the Recovery Control Panel option.

Both the System Rescue Disc and Recovery Drive contain a copy of the Windows Recovery Environment and can be used to start the PC from a state in which you can affect repairs on the boot system.

Sometimes, however, you don't have access to these. If not, then all is not lost. Your Windows install media will permit you to boot to the System Recovery Options, and if you don't have an installation CD/DVD or USB flash drive, you can download an ISO image file that you can burn to disk from the Microsoft TechNet Evaluation Center at http://technet.microsoft.com/evalcenter.

■ **Note** You will need a compatible 32-bit (x86) or 64-bit (x64) System Rescue Disc, Recovery drive, or Windows install media for your system. A 64-bit Recovery drive, for example, cannot be used to rescue a 32-bit Windows installation.

When starting your PC from a Windows installer, click through the language page and at the Install page, click the Repair your computer link, which can be found at the bottom left of the window (see Figure 7-5).

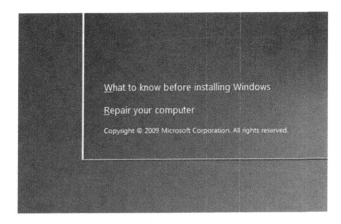

Figure 7-5. *Click Repair your computer to access the Recovery tools*

A System Rescue Disc or Recovery drive will start automatically into its auto-repair mode (see Figure 7-6). Auto-repair works similarly to the automated troubleshooters in the Windows Action Center and can reset Windows components to their default state. This can rectify some startup issues and is well worth trying if you are having difficulty starting a PC. Alternatively, you can click Cancel to access the Recovery tools.

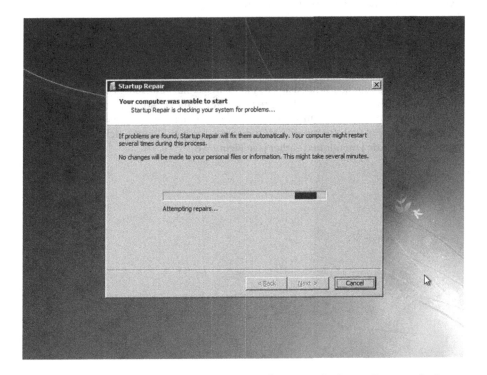

Figure 7-6. *You have to cancel the auto-repair tool to access the System Recovery Options*

It's also possible that you will see the Windows System image recovery tool appear (see Figure 7-7) and prompt you to recover your PC from a system backup you've made previously.

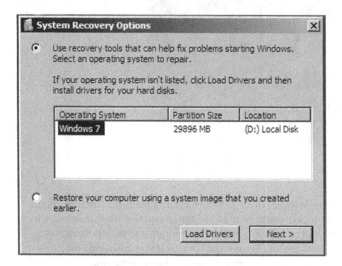

Figure 7-7. The System Recovery Options screen

Should this happen, you must first check the Restore your computer using a system image that you created earlier option, click Next, and at the next screen, click the Cancel button. Should an operating system not appear in the System Recovery Options panel, check the Restore your computer using a system image that you created earlier for more options, including being able to select a recovery image that is stored on a network share.

Whichever route you take to get to the Recovery Options, the menu will eventually offer you a variety of tools for repairing Windows issues, including a quick link to the Memory Diagnostic I mentioned earlier (see Figure 7-8).

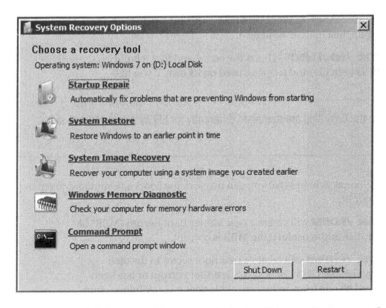

Figure 7-8. *Click Command Prompt in the System Recovery Options panel*

At this panel, you should click Command Prompt, because it's here that the tools you need to repair the Windows boot system can be found.

Rebuilding the Windows Boot Files

The Windows Recovery Environment contains a command-line tool for rebuilding the boot files in Windows. For many tasks, such as when the BCD file has become corrupt, this will do the job perfectly well. To execute this command, type the following into a Command Prompt window.

1. **BcdEdit /export C:\BCD_Backup**—This first command creates a backup copy of the Windows boot files that can later be reimported using the /import switch. The C:\ represents the drive letter of the hard disk or partition you wish to store the file on.

2. **C:**

3. **Cd boot**—This navigates to the boot folder containing the file we have to rebuild.

4. **Attrib bcd -s -h -r**—This command changes the protected flags of the BCD file so that we can rename it.

5. **Ren C:\Boot\bcd C:\Boot\bcd.old**—This renames the BCD file, again, just in case we need it.

6. **Bootrec /rebuildBCD**—This is the command that rebuilds the BCD boot file, and it can be used on its own, if you like.

■ **Note**   Because the boot files are managed differently for EFI systems, you can skip stages 2 to 5.

There are additional switches that you can use with the Bootrec command to repair the boot files on your PC.

- **Bootrec /FixMBR** will create a new Master Boot Record (MBR) file for the disk and is useful if the MBR is corrupt.

- **Bootrec /FixBoot** will create a new boot sector to the disk and can be used if the boot sector is either corrupt or has been replaced by one from an incompatible version of Windows, such as a legacy version, or another OS, such as GNU/Linux.

- **Bootrec /ScanOS** will scan your computer's hard disks for installed operating systems and report on what it finds. This can be useful if the /rebuildBCD switch isn't finding your version of Windows.

In some severe cases, the partitions containing the Windows boot files have themselves become corrupt and have to be rebuilt. You can do this, but you must take extra care when rebuilding these partitions, so as not to damage your Windows or other partitions as well.

In order to rebuild the partitions, they must be re-created at the end of your physical disk. At the Command Prompt, type the following commands, being very careful of your syntax and options:

1. **Diskpart**—to open the disk partitioning tool

2. **List volume**—to display a list of the drives and partitions in your PC

3. **Select volume X**—X represents the number of the volume you wish to shrink, usually the one at the end of the disk on which Windows is installed.

4. **Shrink desired=500**—to shrink the volume by 500MB. This is a good size and can also be used in cases where the Windows System Image Backup system reports it can't operate because there's not enough space on the System Reserved partition.

5. **Create partition primary size=500**—to create a new partition in the blank space available of 500MB

6. **List volume**—to check that you have your new partition, making a note of its volume number

7. **Select volume X**—X represents the volume number for the new partition you have created.

8. **Format quick**—to format this drive using the NTFS file system with default parameters

9. **Assign letter=G**—We must give this new partition a drive letter, so that we can create boot files on it. The List volume command will also detail the drive letters in use on your PC, so change G to the next available letter.

10. **Exit**—to leave the diskpart utility

11. **Dir D:**—just to check your Windows installation is where you think it will be. A copy of Windows installed on the C: drive will normally appear under the D: drive letter when performing this operation.

12. **BcdBoot D:\Windows /s G:**—to copy the Windows boot files from the drive on which Windows is installed to the new partition you have created

13. **Diskpart**—to reenter the disk partitioning utility

14. **Select volume X**—to select the new partition you have created. It will have the same number as before, although you can also type "Select volume G:" to select it, by using its drive letter.

15. **Active**—to make the new partition an active partition

16. **Exit**—to exit diskpart

This procedure has created a new Boot partition for your PC, and this will then show up in the Disk Management console (which you can search for from the Start menu or Start screen) under the drive letter you have assigned it.

It's always a good idea, when you're next at the Windows desktop and can run the Disk Management Console, to remove this drive letter, to hide the partition. To do this, right-click the partition in the Disk Management Console and select Change Drive Letter and Paths. Here, you will find a Remove button for the drive letter.

Manually Repairing the Boot Menu

In some cases, you might find that the boot system is working fine but that it's lost your installed copy of Windows. You can manually edit the boot menu by using the bcdedit command after opening a Command Prompt (Admin) window on the PC.

Typing "BCDEdit" on its own will display a list of the installed operating systems in the boot files (see Figure 7-9).

```
                        Administrator: Command Prompt              –  □  ×
Microsoft Windows [Version 6.3.9600]
(c) 2013 Microsoft Corporation. All rights reserved.

C:\Windows\system32>bcdedit

Windows Boot Manager
--------------------
identifier              {bootmgr}
device                  partition=\Device\HarddiskVolume4
path                    \EFI\Microsoft\Boot\bootmgfw.efi
description             Windows Boot Manager
locale                  en-GB
inherit                 {globalsettings}
integrityservices       Enable
isolatedcontext         Yes
default                 {current}
resumeobject            {dae5d329-0b65-11e4-9fea-a7a1a959d893}
displayorder            {current}
toolsdisplayorder       {memdiag}
timeout                 30

Windows Boot Loader
-------------------
identifier              {current}
device                  partition=C:
path                    \Windows\system32\winload.efi
description             Windows 8.1
locale                  en-GB
inherit                 {bootloadersettings}
recoverysequence        {dae5d32b-0b65-11e4-9fea-a7a1a959d893}
integrityservices       Enable
recoveryenabled         Yes
isolatedcontext         Yes
allowedinmemorysettings 0x15000075
osdevice                partition=C:
systemroot              \Windows
resumeobject            {dae5d329-0b65-11e4-9fea-a7a1a959d893}
nx                      OptIn
bootmenupolicy          Standard
hypervisorlaunchtype    Auto
useplatformclock        Yes
```

Figure 7-9. Reviewing the contents of the BCD file with BCDEdit

Each installed operating system will have its own Globally Unique Identifier (GUID), and in this example, you can see there is one OS installed—Windows 8.1, with the GUID {current} detailed in the Identifier field.

An operating system's GUID could also be expressed as a long hexadecimal string, such as those seen in the recoverysequence and resumeobject fields. You can also use BcdEdit to the switches /enum all, to view your global disk structure.

- **Default {GUID}** sets the default OS entry for the boot options.

- **/export** and **/import** make a backup copy or restore a backup copy of the boot options data.

- **/timeout [num]** changes the time Windows waits for confirmation of which OS you wish to load in dual-boot systems. The value [num] is the number of seconds.

To manually create a new BCD record, i.e., if your Windows installation is not recognized, or if you have to configure a dual-boot system, follow these steps:

1. Open the Command Prompt window from the Recovery Console or, with Administrator rights, from the Windows desktop.

2. In the Command Prompt window, type **BcdEdit /enum all** to show the data for every installed operating system and device in your PC.

3. Type **Bcdedit /export "C:\BCD_Backup"** to create a backup copy of the BCD file, just in case...

4. Type **BcdEdit /create {GUID} /d "OS Name"**, where the {GUID} variable is either the GUID returned by the BCDEdit / enum all command, earlier reported by the BootRec /scanos command, or {legacy}, for Windows XP or an earlier version of Windows.

5. Type **BcdEdit /set {GUID} device partition+D:**, where D: is the drive on which the OS is installed.

6. Type **BcdEdit /set {GUID} path /ntldr**, which is the default path for the OS loader. In GNU/Linux this is called /linux.bin.

7. Type **BcdEdit /displayorder {GUID} /addlast** to add this OS to the end of the current boot menu.

You can also use the following commands with BcdEdit:

- **/set {GUID} Description "OS Name"**—Changes the name of an operating system in the boot list. This can be useful if you have multiple copies of the same OS installed in a dual-boot configuration.

- **/default {GUID}**—Sets the default OS

- **/set {GUID} device partition=X:**—Used when an operating system is shown as being located on the incorrect partition. This sets the correct partition. You *must* then also use the command bcdedit /set {GUID} osdevice partition=X:.

Dual Booting Windows with GNU/Linux

If adding a GNU/Linux OS to the BCD menu doesn't work using the preceding method, you can use a Linux *and* Windows operation to install Windows after Linux has already been installed, which fixes the problem.

1. Open the Linux **Terminal** with root privileges.

2. Type **Fdisk −l** to determine which partition Linux is installed on. This will be listed as /dev/sda1 or /dev/hda1, wherein the number may change.

3. Install the GRUB boot manager by typing **grub-install /dev/ sda1,** making sure you are referencing the partition on which Linux is installed.

4. Copy the Linux boot sector by typing **dd if=/dev/sda1 of / tmp/linux.bin bs=512 count=1.**

5. Manually copy **linux.bin** to a different partition or USB flash drive, to create a backup copy.

6. Install your copy of Windows.

7. Once at the Windows desktop, copy the backup copy of **Linux.bin** to the root (active) partition of your hard disk. If you're not sure what partition this is, from the Command Line (Admin), type **diskpart** and Enter, and to start the disk management tools, type **diskmgmnt.msc** to find out.

8. Create a GRUB entry by typing into a Command Prompt (Admin) window **bcdedit /create /d "GRUB" /application BOOTSECTOR**. This returns a GUID value you should note, as you will need it for the next operations.

9. Type **BcdEdit /set {GUID} device boot.**

10. Type **BcdEdit /set {GUID} PATH /Linux.bin.**

11. Type **BcdEdit /displayOrder {GUID} /addlast.**

Backing Up the Windows Boot Files

Sometimes, it's easier and simpler to keep a backup copy of the boot files for your PC, so that you can restore them at a later date. You can't do this from within Windows, as the OS will prevent you from accessing the System Reserved or EFI System partitions with its security, but you can access them from a portable OS, such as a GNU/Linux bootable CD.

Once in Linux, search for *disk*, to start the Hard Disk Manager, and here, you can mount and view the contents of the System Reserved or EFI System partitions (see Figure 7-10).

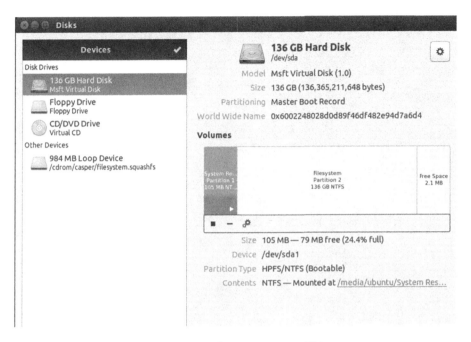

Figure 7-10. *Viewing the System Reserved partition in GNU/Linux*

Here, you can copy all the files from the System Reserved and EFI System partitions to another hard disk or USB flash drive for safe-keeping. They can be copied back at a later stage, by booting from the GNU/Linux CD again.

It's worth noting that Linux distros also include partition-management utilities that, in some but not all cases, can be used to repair a damaged boot partition.

Summary

The Windows boot system is designed to be inaccessible and difficult to work with. This is all part of Microsoft's work to keep rootkit viruses out of the partitions and why the system was changed so radically from legacy versions of Windows.

Windows is still a series of files running on fairly standard hardware however, with good compatibility for other operating systems. This means it's still fairly easy to make low-level changes when needs be, in order to repair problems and troubleshoot more serious issues.

CHAPTER 8

■ ■ ■

Restoring Files and Folder Security Settings

Many years ago, when I was a junior sysadmin, my experienced IT manager said to me, "Administrative privileges have to be earned and not taken for granted." I think he was trying to protect me (and more, important, his workplace) from the potential damage that a noob administrator can wreak if he or she is not careful! We can all sometimes take the administrator account that we use for granted.

Accidents can and will happen from time to time, and when brought on by an administrator, they are often more spectacular in their effect. For example, you may perhaps perform a task directly on a production machine rather than a lab environment, or add the wrong switch to a command prompt utility and nuke a system. In this short chapter, we will explore methods of recovering a system that has suffered from losing New Technology File System (NTFS) file and folder permissions.

What Can Go Wrong?

In earlier chapters, we provided guidance, best practice, and troubleshooting tips. One piece of advice related to removing inherited NTFS file permission from a folder. This can lead to no permissions remaining on the folder hierarchy in question. No permissions means no access for anyone, even administrators!

Other issues that can cause permissions to go awry include registry corruption— SMB share permissions are stored in the registry. Malware is a prime candidate for attacking the %windir%\system32 folder and will prevent access or lock out Windows or your anti-malware tools to perform cleanup tasks. Windows Defender and User Account Control (UAC) are valuable features within Windows that have been significant factors in reducing the damage caused by malware in modern versions of Windows, but many users (especially home users) continue to ignore onscreen warnings and will readily provide administrator-level access whenever an installer requests it. It is good that in an enterprise everyone is a standard user!

© Mike Halsey and Andrew Bettany 2015
M. Halsey and A. Bettany, *Windows File System Troubleshooting*,
DOI 10.1007/978-1-4842-1016-1_8

We learn by experimenting with file permissions—we actually have to lock ourselves out. This helps to reinforce the concepts. It is hoped that permission-related meltdowns will be confined to a virtual machine lab environment. A lab will afford you some protection while you are experimenting or practicing configuring share and NTFS permissions. While working in a virtual lab, from time to time, you should take a checkpoint of the working system. As shown in Figure 8-1, I have taken a checkpoint (previously known as a snapshot) of my Windows 8.1 VM running, using Hyper-V on my Surface Pro 3, prior to performing some of the tasks covered later in this chapter.

Figure 8-1. *Taking a checkpoint in Hyper-V*

Should anything happen to my VM that I cannot resolve quickly, I can apply a previously created checkpoint, and I will revert to a fully working system within a matter of seconds. Virtualization technology is awesome.

If you are not working in a virtual machine, and if your computer suffers a complete meltdown, recovering the system can be a little more time-consuming.

Symptoms and Remedies

The typical symptoms of a (previously responsive) system that is suffering from incorrectly or overly restrictive file security settings could result in the following symptoms:

- Application startup failures

- Slow system response when accessing folders and files

- Authentication or authorization failures

In my experience within a managed domain environment, the causes of the problem are often not easy to diagnose, as, frequently, a user will suffer one or more of the symptoms and not report the problem to the help desk. We generally train users to "self-diagnose," and sometimes they can become desensitized over time and believe that all their issues relate to the "network being slow" or a similar common IT problem. Often, they will try to self-cure, by restarting their workstation. Conversely, if an issue with one of the symptoms listed is reported to the help desk, then, unfortunately, the help desk may suggest that the problem relates to users having too many applications open or, also, a slowness in the network causing delays in accessing resources across the network. The overall effect is a Catch-22 situation whereby the effectiveness and productivity suffers.

The following tasks, when deployed incorrectly, can result in poorly configured security settings:

- Group Policy changes

- Operating system upgrades and service pack installations

- Illicit, aborted, or incomplete system restorations, operating system cloning

- Application upgrades and installations

- Deployment of security templates

- Modifications to User Rights assignments

- Modification of security settings in Active Directory or the Registry

- Modification of file permissions the file system or the Registry

- Malware attack on one or several of these settings

Often, there is a mismatch between local, remote, or centralized settings, whereby the operating system struggles to resolve the correct permission state, causing the system responsiveness to be less than normal.

One method by which the help desk can diagnose the issue is to request that the user attempt to re-create the problem on a clean installation/newly deployed computer that is part of the corporate network. This will normally establish if the issue is local or relates to a central configuration.

Table 8-1 outlines some of the potential methods that could be used to restore a Windows installation to a previously working state. We have excluded the option of reinstalling the operating system.

Table 8-1. *NTFS Permission Reset Methods*

Method	Description	Suitability
File Explorer	Manually reset files and folders using administrative privileges	Useful for very low volume. Impractical and inefficient to scale
Windows Backup	Used to restore full or partial data structures	Slow to complete, reliable
System Restore	Creates system state backups but excludes file and folder permissions	Allows rollback of OS to a prior time only
icacls	Command-line tool. Used to set or reset NTFS permissions on files/folders to default settings	Easy to use, quick and efficient. Ideal for specific folders
Takeown	Command-line tool. Reassigns NTFS ownership	Easy to use, quick and efficient, though may interfere with quotas

Resetting Permissions

Let's assume that you decided to remove all of the permissions from a sensitive file that you created, and the permissions looked like those shown in the access control list (ACL) in Figure 8-2. When you try to launch the file, you receive an error stating that "Access is denied."

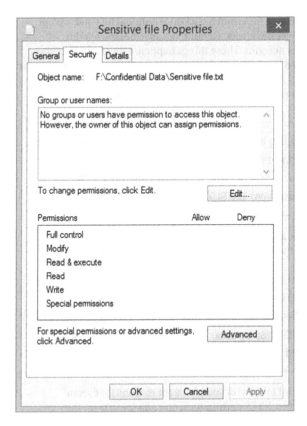

Figure 8-2. *ACL displaying no permissions*

To resolve this mistake, you can simply modify the file permissions again, using File Explorer, and add your name to the ACL and allocate yourself some permissions. You can then access the file again. All should be good.

▪ **Note**   One of the by-products of removing all NTFS permissions from a file is that it is nearly impossible for anyone to rename, modify, or even delete the file.

The problems for a sysadmin become challenging when an ex-employee either deletes his/her files or removes all the permissions from his/her own files before leaving. If you also deleted the user account, rather than disabling it, you will have your work cut out.

You will have to restore the deleted files from a backup. All should be good, except that the "owner" of the files no longer has a user account, because he/she left the company, and you deleted the user account. These things happen, especially in smaller organizations that are not regulated by the Health Insurance Portability and Accountability Act (HIPAA) or the Sarbanes-Oxley Act (SOX), which now legally forces many corporations to have procedures and policies in place to ensure data protection and accountability.

■ **Note**   For more information relating to how HIPAA or SOX placed huge responsibilities on corporations in relation to securing data, auditing, and accountability, review the links www.hhs.gov/ocr/privacy/hipaa/understanding/srsummary.html (for HIPAA) and www.sec.gov/about/laws.shtml#sox2002 (for SOX).

Even if you create a fresh new account for a deleted user account, Windows will re-create a new unique SID, and, therefore, the ACLs will not apply to the new user.

■ **Tip**   If you are prone to deleting user accounts in Active Directory, it may be worth investigating the Active Directory Recycle Bin feature, available since Windows Server 2008 R2. You can manage this feature with ease by using the Active Directory Administrative Center in Windows Server 2012 and newer versions.

If you get locked out of files and folders on your drive for reasons that seem to originate from incorrect or deleted NTFS permissions, you can try to reset the permissions back to their default settings, using the icacls tool. You can perform this directly from an administrative command prompt in Windows 8, and all objects (folders and files) that are inherited from the root directory will be returned to their default out-of-the-box state.

To test this procedure on your lab environment, navigate to the root of the folder or drive that contains your demo files and folder and then type the following command into an administrative command prompt, as shown in Figure 8-3:

```
icacls * /RESET /T /C /Q
```

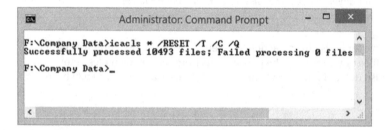

Figure 8-3. *Reset NTFS permissions using* icacls

The process is quick and efficient. On my test system, the command reset 10,493 files in less than 15 seconds. Because the tool will reset the permissions to the original operating system defaults, you should be very careful to use only the tool on the specific folders. Remember: This tool does not restore **your** original bespoke/customized NTFS settings. It restores the default file and folder permissions and inheritance, which will then allow you to access the files again. You should then reapply the necessary permissions, so that the files are secured again, according to your corporate policy.

The syntax for resetting the ACLs back to their defaults using icacls is icacls Name /Reset [/T] [/C] [/L] [/Q], as shown in Table 8-2.

Table 8-2. *Using* icacls *to Reset NTFS File Permissions*

Command Switch	Description
icacls	Displays or modifies discretionary access control lists (DACLs) on specified files
/RESET	Replaces ACLs with default inherited ACLs for all matching files
/T	Performs the operation on all specified files in the current directory and its subdirectories
/C	Continue despite any file errors. Error messages will be displayed.
/Q	Suppresses success messages

Taking Back Ownership

If the user account was deleted but the remaining permissions are still valid, you may have only either to take ownership or grant the ownership to another user. We would continue to use the icacls tool, and the following command:

Icacls * /setowner "Administrators" /T /C

Another built-in command-line tool that will also enable an administrator to recover access to a file is the Takeown utility. The syntax for the tool is

Takeown [/s <Computer> [/u [<Domain>\]<User name> [/p [<Password>]]]] /f <File name> [/a] [/r [/d {Y|N}]]

The switch parameters for the Takeown tool are shown in Table 8-3.

Table 8-3. *Syntax of the Takeown Command-Line Tool*

Command Switch	Description
Takeown	Enables an administrator to recover access to a file that previously was denied, by making the administrator the owner of the file
/s <Computer>	Specifies the remote computer. Default value is the local computer.
/u [<Domain>\]<User name>	Runs the tool with the permissions of the specified user account or the system permission (default)
/p [<Password>]	Specifies the password of the user account that is specified in the /u parameter
/f <File name>	Specifies the file name or directory name. Wildcards are allowed.
/a	Allocates ownership to the Administrators group
/r	Performs recursive operations on all files and files in sub-folders
/d {Y | N}	Suppresses confirmation prompt
/?	Displays help

icacls and Takeown are not ideal for all situations, and the full reset of permissions is quite heavy-handed, if you are seeking only to restore a small component of your settings. You would not wish to run the full icacls reset anywhere near a file server.

System Restore

Although still supported, though slightly out of favor with Windows 8 and newer operating systems, the System Restore feature, as shown in Figure 8-4, offers some relief, if the cause of your lost permissions relates to malware or application installation issues. Unfortunately, this tool will only restore the system state and registry, and it is not able to restore corrupted files and folders or NTFS permissions. They will remain untouched by the process. One of the benefits of performing a system restore is that it is nondestructive to files.

Figure 8-4. *Manually creating a system restore point*

Since Windows 7, System Restore has been improved, and the feature will advise you of any applications that might be affected by running the restore process. This is relevant to only the recent applications, i.e., those that have been installed or updated since the last restore point was made.

■ **Note**   System Restore is not enabled by default. You have to enable system protection for the drives on your computer before you are able to use System Restore.

So, if the tool does not help restore NTFS permissions, why is it included in this section? Good question. Even though the System Restore feature will not reinstate your file permissions (or even restore deleted files), it still has the ability to help us, should our system become infected by malware. Reverting Windows to a known system restore point, let's say yesterday, when, for example, you believe that your PC was not affected by malware, allows you to clean the malware off your system before it has become "active," i.e., before it is installed and has configured Windows with various startup settings that will cause malware applications to run.

The System Restore feature is located in the System control panel applet. To turn on or configure System Restore on a Windows 8 device, you should type **recovery** into the Start screen and then select Recovery, to display the Advanced recovery tools screen shown in Figure 8-5.

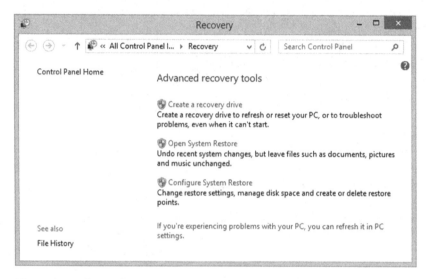

Figure 8-5. *Advanced recovery tools, including System Restore*

Any file permission damage that may have occurred may still be present, but restoring file permissions is a lot easier without the malware software trying to thwart your efforts, often undoing your actions every time you reboot. Once "clean," you can then reapply NTFS permissions using the icacls tool.

■ **Note** System Restore will not remove the actual malware executable files. You will still have to remove these, or if it was included in an e-mail, you will still have to delete the malware infected e-mail yourself.

Simply resetting NTFS permissions may not help you, especially if you cannot even boot the device to Windows. In those situations, you should consider repairing your Windows installation using a portable OS, which is discussed in the next chapter.

Summary

We have seen how to reset and restore file level permissions which are useful for when members of staff leave the organisation with their files in a locked down state. For tackling configuration and installation errors or even virus infections we can use the hidden gem of System Restore to teleport the OS back to a prior system state.

Throughout this book we have introduced many tools and tips for you to recover your system, many of the built into Windows. We take a slightly out of the box approach to repairing your system in Chapter 9, by using a portable OS installed on an external drive which allows us to bypass much of the security that we have been discussing throughout the book.

CHAPTER 9

■ ■ ■

Repairing the Windows File System Using a Portable OS

So far in this book, we've detailed how you can manage and audit file and folder ownership and security permissions; overall disk and file security; encryption; troubleshooting disk, file, and system errors; and how to repair, automatically or manually, the Windows boot system.

You could still find yourself in a situation, however, in which, even though the boot system is operational, Windows itself is corrupt to the point where you can't get to the desktop to repair files.

In this circumstance, the immediate reaction might be to reimage and reinstall the PC. Certainly, in a corporate environment, this is the norm; however, if you know, or at least have a fair understanding, of what's gone wrong, it can still be quicker to repair the problem itself.

You can achieve this by replacing corrupt files on the computer's hard disk with ones from the original Windows installer image—and I'll show you how to do this shortly— from the original driver file, and so on. It should be noted, though, that, especially in Windows, file versions do change when updates and service packs are installed, and so, while you should always use a Windows install image that includes the latest service pack that's installed on the PC, there are still no guarantees the corrupt file hadn't also been updated afterward by Windows Update.

Accessing the Contents of the Windows install.wim File

In Windows 7 and Windows 8.1, the operating system is installed from an image file, called install.wim, which is simply unpacked from the installation media to the computer's hard disk. This helps speed the update process, being faster than a file-by-file copy, but it also creates a valuable resource from which you can unpick one or several Windows OS files, enabling you to replace individual files on a computer's hard disk, should they become corrupt.

Legacy versions of Windows included an install disk that contained all of the Windows component files in either an uncompressed format or inside a Windows

© Mike Halsey and Andrew Bettany 2015
M. Halsey and A. Bettany, *Windows File System Troubleshooting*,
DOI 10.1007/978-1-4842-1016-1_9

Cabinet (.cab) file container, which is rather like a zip file and can be opened by ZIP management software such as WinZip and WinRAR.

With Windows Vista, Microsoft wanted to greatly speed up the installation process and created the install.wim file (see Figure 9-1).

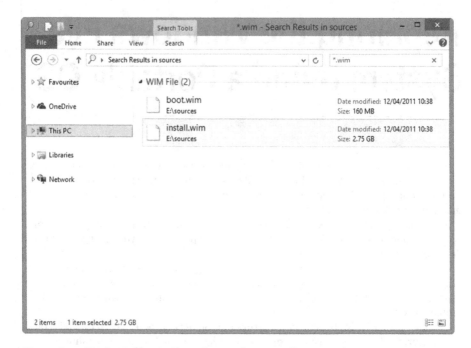

Figure 9-1. The install.wim file in the Windows installation media

A .wim file is a Windows Image and, just as it sounds, is an image just like an ISO file you might download from Microsoft to burn a Windows installation disk. The purpose of the install.wim file is to have a copy of the core operating system (OS) files that can be simply unpacked as is to the destination hard disk, thus speeding up the install process.

Unlike an ISO file, however, you can't mount a WIM file in File Explorer (Windows Explorer in Windows Vista and Windows 7) so that you can view and manage its contents, but you can still access what's inside.

To do this, you'll require a utility from Microsoft, and the one you choose will vary, depending on which version of the OS you're going to be working with.

- For Windows Vista, download the Windows Automated Installation Kit (AIK) from http://pcs.tv/1DxMJ7d.

- For Windows 7, download AIK for Windows 7 from http://pcs.tv/1w8xY10.

- For Windows 8, download the Assessment and Deployment Toolkit (ADK) from http://pcs.tv/1BVdnCM.

> ■ **Note** In fairness, to just access the contents of a .wim file, you can use any of these AIKs
> or the ADK, as the process is the same. As you'll be administering systems, however, it's a good
> idea to download and install the one most relevant to the version of Windows you have installed.

Once the AIK or ADK is installed, copy the install.wim file from your installation
DVD, USB flash drive, or mounted ISO file to your hard disk. You will also have to create
an empty folder in which to extract the contents of the .wim file.

From your Start menu or Start screen, run the Deployment Tools Command Prompt
as an Administrator, and in the command window that appears, type the following:

```
Imagex /mount f:\install.wim 2 d:\wim8
```

This changes the locations of the install.wim file on your PC and the destination
folder you wish to extract it to (see Figure 9-2).

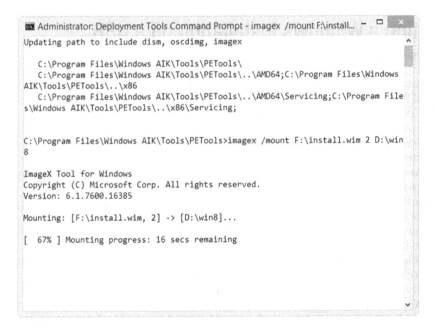

Figure 9-2. *Extracting a WIM file to a PC*

This command will extract the contents of the WIM file with read-only access, and
you can copy these files and replace those in a faulty Windows installation, as required.

Should you wish to extract the contents of the WIM file with read/write access, use
the following command instead:

```
Imagex /mountrw f:\install.wim 2 d:\win8
```

You will now have a copy on your hard disk of the core Windows OS files. Should any of these have become corrupted, you can copy the original file back, and I'll detail the method by which you can do this shortly.

■ **Note**   It's worth noting here that should you have a service pack installed on your PC, some of the core OS files might have changed. This means that the install disk or image you extract the `install.wim` file from should have that service pack integrated within it. You can download ISO files containing service packs if you are a Microsoft Developer Network (MSDN) subscriber or have Software Assurance benefits through volume licencing. Should neither of these apply, there are tools you can find online to integrate service packs into your installation ISO file, such as the excellent RT7Lite. These vary by Windows version but can be found by searching online.

Creating a Windows Installation on a USB Flash Drive

When you come to manually repair files in your Windows installation, you will have to start your PC from a portable OS. In an enterprise environment, this could be using a recovery disk, such as using the Emergency Recovery Disk that is part of the Diagnostics and Recovery Toolkit (DaRT). Alternative tools for non-enterprise customers include the Hirens Boot CD (`www.hiren.info/pages/bootcd`) or BartPE (`www.nu2.nu/pebuilder/`).

A little unconventional, but still useful, is the Windows To Go (WTG) drive. If you are appropriately licensed, you could use a USB drive preloaded with a functional installation of Windows 8. WTG is a feature available in the Enterprise version of Windows 8. However, the security built into the Windows To Go drive will prevent you from accessing any of the hard disks on the host PC. To manually override this and access the local drives, you will have to allocate the host drives a drive letter within Disk Management.

Even if you do not possess a supported WTG drive, and you can find a list of compatible drives at `http://pcs.tv/1G0aB6V`, you can create a Windows To Go–style USB flash drive using any Windows OS (Vista, Windows 7, or Windows 8), and the OS you use has no bearing on the OS you're rescuing, so a Windows 8 portable drive can be used to rescue Windows Vista on the hard disk and vice versa.

The supported drives have extremely fast read/write characteristics. While you can perform the following task using a standard USB drive, you will find that the performance is poor. You will need a USB flash drive of 32GB or larger and a valid product key for the edition of Windows you are going to use. Alternatively, if you will be creating a USB flash drive only to use once, you can download a trial copy of Windows from the Microsoft TechNet Evaluation Center at `http://technet.microsoft.com/evalcenter`.

To create your portable Windows OS, open a Command Prompt window as Administrator and type the following commands:

1. **Diskpart**—To run the Windows disk partitioning tool

2. **List disk**—To view all the disks in your PC. Make a note of the disk number for your USB flash drive.

3. **Select disk 2**—Where the number will change to represent your USB flash drive

4. **Clean**—Prepares the drive for formatting

5. **Create partition primary**—Creates a new partition on the cleaned disk

6. **Format fs=ntfs quick**—Formats this new partition

7. **Active**—To mark the new partition as active and bootable

8. **Assign letter=e**—We need to temporarily assign a drive letter to the disk, so that we can install Windows onto it.

9. **Exit**—To exit diskpart

10. Now, either mount a Windows ISO image file or insert an install DVD or USB flash drive into your PC.

11. **Dism /apply-image /imagefile=f:\sources\install.wim /index:1 /applydir:e:**—Where f: is the drive containing your Windows install media and e: is the newly prepared USB flash drive

12. **Bceboot.exe e:\windows /w e: /f ALL**—To set the new USB flash drive as bootable

When you next start the PC from the USB flash drive, Windows will install to it. It's wise to perform this process on the PC you need to rescue, as Windows will install drivers specific to that hardware. Creating a portable Windows drive on a PC with BIOS firmware and then trying to use it on another PC with EFI firmware (and vice versa) can also cause problems, because the Windows boot files might be incompatible with the PC.

Once Windows is installed on the USB flash drive and you have booted the PC from it, you will be able to use it to see, access, and modify the files on the host PC's hard disk.

Having a bootable copy of Windows on a USB flash drive also presents the benefit of being able to install software onto that flash drive. This could include diagnostic and repair software, such as the Microsoft SysInternals Suite, antivirus or anti-rootkit software, or any other diagnostic and repair package you can otherwise install onto a Windows PC.

Repairing Windows Files Using a GNU/Linux Disk

Perhaps slightly easier than creating a portable Windows USB flash drive is the use of a GNU/Linux CD, and any Linux distro will be fine for this purpose—or a bootable disk, such as Hirens or the BartPE that I mentioned earlier in this chapter, that will allow you access to the file system on the host PC. GNU/Linux will be most familiar to people, though, so let's spend some time looking at how we can use a Linux distro to repair a damaged Windows environment.

Linux has long had the advantage of allowing you to burn an ISO to a disk and to run Linux directly from that disk without the need to install the OS itself. The upshot of this is that, as you can see in Figure 9-3, you can view, edit, and modify all the files on the host PC from the Linux file explorer, as well as perform additional tasks, such as managing partitions.

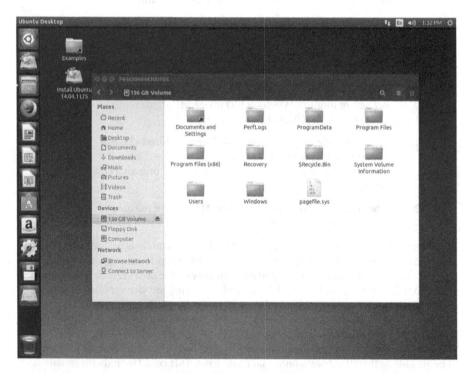

Figure 9-3. *You can view and edit the contents of your Windows drive using GNU/Linux*

If you have to replace any Windows files, such as those you have extracted from an install.wim file or copied from another PC with an identical installation, you can do so here.

It's also worth noting that, should you have problems with the Windows, System Reserved, or EFI System partitions, GNU/Linux ISOs come equipped with their own partition management tools, and in Figure 9-4, you can see the GParted tool in Ubuntu.

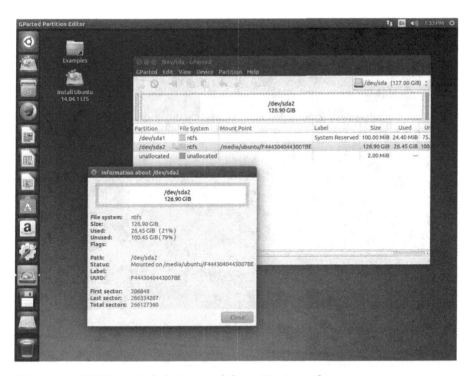

Figure 9-4. *GNU/Linux includes its own disk partitioning tools*

So How Do You Know What to Repair?

It's all well and good being able to access the Windows files on your PC to repair them, but how do you know what to repair?

You might receive a Blue Screen of Death (BSOD) message (see Figures 9-5 and 9-6). Should a file be at fault, the BSOD will inform you (SPCMDCON.SYS and pci.sys being the offending files in the two examples shown).

A problem has been detected and Windows has been shut down to prevent damage
to your computer.

The problem seems to be caused by the following file: SPCMDCON.SYS

PAGE_FAULT_IN_NONPAGED_AREA

If this is the first time you've seen this Stop error screen,
restart your computer. If this screen appears again, follow
these steps:

Check to make sure any new hardware or software is properly installed.
If this is a new installation, ask your hardware or software manufacturer
for any Windows updates you might need.

If problems continue, disable or remove any newly installed hardware
or software. Disable BIOS memory options such as caching or shadowing.
If you need to use Safe Mode to remove or disable components, restart
your computer, press F8 to select Advanced Startup Options, and then
select Safe Mode.

Technical information:

*** STOP: 0x00000050 (0xFD3094C2,0x00000001,0xFBFE7617,0x00000000)

*** SPCMDCON.SYS - Address FBFE7617 base at FBFE5000, DateStamp 3d6dd67c

Figure 9-5. The Blue Screen of Death can provide useful information

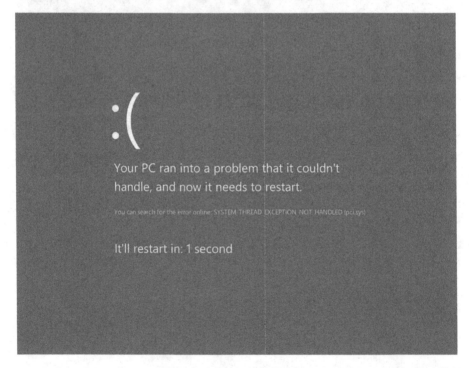

Figure 9-6. The Windows 8 BSOD also informs you if the fault is related to an offending file

If there are issues with the Windows or boot partitions, and they have become corrupt, these issues can be repaired using a portable OS such as GNU/Linux, which sometimes includes its own partition management and repair tools.

Creating a custom Windows USB flash drive from which you can boot the PC allows you to install additional win32 diagnostic and repair software onto that flash drive, such as partition management, antivirus, and anti-rootkit software. These last two can be used to scan the disks, including system partitions of the underlying PC, for malware.

If you are experiencing the problem since installing a software package or hardware driver, then you'll have a good idea where to start, and a search online can often reveal all of the file names for the package you have to remove.

Summary

Even if Windows is completely corrupt, there might not be any need to reimage or reinstall the PC (although in an enterprise environment, it may be the preferred option). It could be the case that copying the contents of the install.wim folder back to the PC to replace any corrupt files, removing a program file or driver that has been reported by a Blue Screen of Death as being corrupt, or repairing a problem with the Windows partition structure can get your PC working again.

Regardless of how complex the Windows file structure might be, there are always straightforward ways to repair the OS on a file-by-file basis, if none of the other repair methods we've detailed in this book has worked or is appropriate.

The aim, as always, will be to get the PC up and running again in the shortest possible time, so having a good understanding of the different problems you may face, and the ways in which you can repair them, can only help your standing as an IT professional.

Index

© Mike Halsey and Andrew Bettany 2015
M. Halsey and A. Bettany, *Windows File System Troubleshooting*,
DOI 10.1007/978-1-4842-1016-1

Printed in the United States
By Bookmasters